THE TEACHER EVALUATION
HANDBOOK

THE TEACHER EVALUATION HANDBOOK

Step-by-Step Techniques and Forms for Improving Instruction

Renfro C. Manning

PRENTICE HALL
Englewood Cliffs, New Jersey 07632

Prentice-Hall International (UK) Limited, *London*
Prentice-Hall of Australia Pty. Limited, *Sydney*
Prentice-Hall Canada, Inc., *Toronto*
Prentice-Hall Hispanoamericana, S.A., *Mexico*
Prentice-Hall of India Private Limited, *New Delhi*
Prentice-Hall of Japan, Inc., *Tokyo*
Simon & Schuster Asia Pte. Ltd., *Singapore*
Editora Prentice-Hall do Brasil, Ltda., *Rio de Janeiro*

© 1988 *by*

PRENTICE HALL

Englewood Cliffs, NJ

10 9 8 7 6 5 4 3 2 1

Library of Congress Cataloging-in-Publication Data

Manning, Renfro C.
  The teacher evaluation handbook.

  Bibliography: p.
  Includes index.
  1. Teachers—United States—Rating of—Handbooks,
manuals, etc.   I. Title.
LB2838.M37   1988   371.1'44   88-12500
ISBN 0-13-888389-0

ISBN 0-13-888389-0

PRENTICE HALL
BUSINESS & PROFESSIONAL DIVISION
A division of Simon & Schuster
Englewood Cliffs, New Jersey 07632

Printed in the United States of America

*Dedicated to Sandy
and our children, Clark, Tracy, and Stephanie,
for their support and patience.*

ABOUT THE AUTHOR

Renfro C. Manning is Superintendent of Orange County Public Schools, Orange, Virginia. He is currently President of the Virginia Association of School Administrators. He received the Ed.D. degree from the University of Virginia. Dr. Manning has taught various graduate courses in a broad range of educational topics. He is a frequent consultant and has published in such areas as principal and teacher evaluation and incentive pay for teachers. The Orange County Public Schools has one of the Nation's exemplary pay for performance programs for teachers.

ABOUT THIS BOOK

The purpose of *The Teacher Evaluation Handbook* is to provide a model for developing an effective procedure for teacher evaluation. The material in this book is the result of research, practical experience, failures, and uplifting successes. The main premise is to provide suggested procedures to guide you in developing an evaluation system specifically tailored to meet local needs. There is also information about related issues, such as current trends and evaluation philosophy.

A major part of *The Teacher Evaluation Handbook* is directed toward designing an evaluation system that will:

- impact upon the instructional process
- increase teacher involvement and ownership
- positively affect morale

Traditionally, evaluation is designed for two purposes: to measure quality and to provide a guide for growth or change. These two purposes are discussed in detail.

- Chapter 1 is the first step in a systematic effort to have an effective evaluative system. It offers background information on two types of evaluation: summative and formative. You are given examples of these evaluation systems, and the advantages and disadvantages of both.
- Who and what should be evaluated are discussed in Chapter 2. If you want to upgrade an existing system of evaluation or construct an entirely new system, the information in this chapter will be the starting point.
- Chapter 3 explains how a school or school system can train evaluators. You are given details from selecting peer observers to compensating them for their services.
- How to train observers is covered in Chapter 4. In order for peer evaluators to contribute meaningfully to the evaluation process, a training program must be of high priority.

- Chapter 5 suggests ways for making staff development an important aspect of evaluation. For this to be properly accomplished, a different way of viewing curriculum planning must be adopted. Other practical aspects of staff development are also discussed in this chapter, such as purpose and how to make staff development work.

- The primary tool of evaluation is the conference. Chapter 6 describes the kinds of conferences you can conduct, as well as the most important do's and don'ts of evaluation conferences.

- Evaluation is most productive when used to assist the competent. However, not all teachers are competent, so Chapter 7 is a good place to begin when inadequate performance becomes a problem and winning takes on a new meaning. You will learn the necessary steps for documenting complaints against teachers and being an effective witness at due process hearings.

- An evaluation program, based on teaching practices supported by current research, is a prerequisite for a program of differentiated pay. Chapter 8 is devoted to practical suggestions for designing such a program. Also included is a description of a successful differentiated pay program.

- Summative evaluation, whose purpose is a quick view of teaching quality and to show a need for formal evaluation, is discussed in Chapter 9. Here you will learn how to identify those teachers who need summative evaluation and how to design a summative instrument.

- Chapter 10 "puts it all together" by offering you final considerations in developing an effective evaluation system.

Many useful figures, ready-to-use forms, and checklists can be found throughout the book to help you establish your own evaluation program. An appendix and bibliography are also included to offer new ideas and insights.

The evaluation system can become a powerful tool for working effectively with teachers and students. Whether you want to create a teacher evaluation program or improve an existing one, *The Teacher Evaluation Handbook* will help develop the model for success.

Renfro C. Manning

ACKNOWLEDGMENTS

Many colleagues, outstanding professionals in the Orange County (Virginia) School System, contributed through a willingness to try new ideas and provide challenging insights. Their commitment and devotion to duty led to the overriding theme in this book, which is: change in education requires a change in perception of how to work effectively with teachers and students.

CONTENTS

CHAPTER 9   SUMMATIVE EVALUATIONS   **143**

CHAPTER 10   PUTTING IT ALL TOGETHER   **157**

chapter 1

EVALUATION—GROWTH OR HARASSMENT?

Traditionally, teacher evaluation procedures have been designed around teacher characteristics thought to be desirable, and these characteristics have been measured with checklists of numerical choices to indicate the degree of accomplishment. Although this method of evaluation was devised more than seventy years ago and even though there has been some improvement in the teacher characteristics sought, the checklist or rating scale evaluation in use today remains very similar to that of the early systems. The research that has become widely available in the last decade has made the checklist system of evaluation somewhat obsolete. This is cause for concern, since the use of an obsolete system of evaluation may hinder the adoption of effective teaching practices.

The chief reason that obsolete methods of teacher evaluation remain in use is that the purpose of evaluation is confused. Of course, an uninformed public and overzealous politicians have contributed to the problem. An examination of some traditional purposes of evaluation include the following:

1. Making tenure decisions
2. Determining pay increases
3. Assuring accountability
4. Removing the incompetent
5. Enhancing administrative authority
6. Awarding promotions

Most of the purposes listed above are not viewed in a positive sense by the teaching staff. Moreover, the most important purpose of evaluation, and perhaps the most positive, was not listed—*the improvement of instructional practice.* There is a tendency to fold all purposes of evaluation, including the improvement of instruction, into a single instrument. Once this is done, an attempt to improve the evaluation process may become simply a quest to find the right checklist.

It is doubtful that a procedure designed to help make decisions regarding pay increases, tenure, and promotions can be effective as a tool for improving instruction. This chapter is devoted to suggesting methods to renew the evaluation process. Its primary goal is to demonstrate how evaluation can be transformed from a process often viewed as harassment, by those it is designed to assist, to a process which accommodates both the need to measure and the need to promote growth.

THE USE OF FORMATIVE AND SUMMATIVE EVALUATION

It would be unlikely to give the final examination to the class before instruction begins, but this routinely happens to teachers, and they are expected to improve in the process.

Both summative and formative evaluations have a vital place in the evaluation of teaching. It can be observed from Figure 1-1 that the purposes of

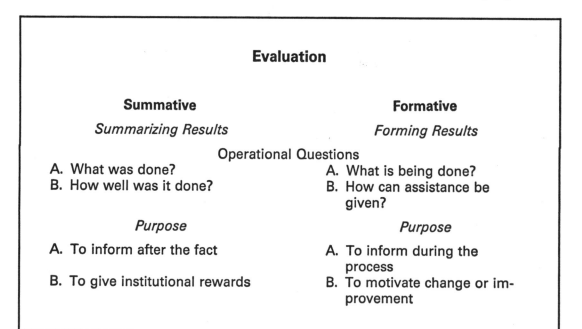

Figure 1-1 Purposes of Evaluation.

formative and summative evaluation are different. Each will be discussed in detail.

Summative

Summative evaluation represents measurement of what has occurred. This quality of measurement of results gives summative evaluation much appeal to those who perceive evaluation as primarily concerned with collecting information— information upon which to base personnel decisions. This after-the-fact aspect of summative evaluation limits the amount of change which can be expected from its use.

An easy way to visualize the limits of summative evaluation is to consider the following discussion of testing in the teaching process:

> Good teaching involves, among other things, some type of preassessment in order that instructional strategies may be devised. Then, as instruction progresses, various sampling processes are employed to assess learning, to reteach, or to alter the instructional procedures. Finally, an initial test may result in some reteaching. At the conclusion of instruction, a test to make final decisions about grading, placement, or promotion is administered; this final assessment is the summative test. There is little or no expectancy that the summative test will have an impact upon learning. The utility of the summative test is to determine what the student has learned.

The function of the summative test is clear in this brief summary of the teaching process. The purposes of summative procedures in teaching are analogous to the summative procedures used in teacher evaluation—the need to grade, place, or promote. These are status decisions.

Formative

Formative evaluation is used to sample the process of learning or improvement, and to help in decision making concerning how the outcome might be improved. In the best sense, formative evaluation must be nonthreatening to the recipient. It must be designed to assist those being evaluated to adopt performance strategies which will result in growth and increased effectiveness.

In the teaching analogy, all activities leading to the final test were formative. They were designed to have an impact upon the end result by sampling growth and guiding the growth process.

MIXING FORMATIVE AND SUMMATIVE EVALUATION

Mixing formative and summative evaluation in the evaluation of teachers is a problem. Most administrators and teachers have a clear concept of the role of summative and formative evaluation; however, it is easy to find a teacher evaluation system with summative components mixed throughout, one composed of summative components exclusively, or one with formative information used for summative documentation. While it would be unlikely to give the final examination to students before instruction begins, this routinely happens to teachers—and they are expected to grow in the process. Of course, growth frequently is not the end result when purposes are "mixed."

Often teachers become confused about the purpose of evaluation when formative and summative procedures are randomly included or when there is an attempt to use summative results to promote growth. The chief problem is credibility. The administration may contend that its purpose is the promotion of growth, but the teachers see a different purpose served when they observe documenting for purposes not clearly articulated.

ELIMINATING THE PROBLEM OF DUAL PURPOSES

Both formative (growth) and summative (accountability) evaluations can be combined in a single instrument, or two instruments can be used. Using two evaluative instruments is the recommended way to keep purposes separate. In the text that follows, each aspect of evaluation will be discussed as if separate procedures were used.

The Growth Process

Formative evaluation should begin early in the school year. A positive protocol should be used for formative evaluations. With a positive protocol, formative observers may use a list of practices required for effective teaching. The observation of effective practices is compiled in an anecdotal record form. The absence of documentation for a practice indicates that it was not observed. For most teachers, the lack of documentation is an ample indication that work needs to be accomplished.

The positive protocol helps ensure that the evaluation procedure remains formative. It also helps to avoid a characteristic of human nature which nullifies many efforts to make evaluation a growth experience. This nullifying characteristic is the tendency of teachers to overreact to negative input. The result is not growth, but hostility, rationalization, embarrassment, and avoidance.

From the beginning of the school year, formative evaluations should proceed on a periodic basis. Growth records can be kept, and a reward system can be utilized at the end of the year. Teachers can then respond to recognition, autonomy, and professional growth. Any plan to reward should incorporate these qualities. Of course, the teacher should know whether a formative or summative process is being used.

Accountability

The summative evaluations can summarize what was observed and what was not observed. It is preferable to use an anecdotal record that follows a set protocol and outlines expected performance. Those who use a summative procedure may prefer that both positive performance and needed improvement be stated by the evaluator. This evaluation should be done by personnel other than those involved in the formative process. The principal is the key person in the summative process. In addition to the principal, subject-matter supervisors and other supervisory personnel may be involved. Summative evaluation is usually preceded with several observations. Prior to the end of the year, a summative conference is conducted.

When there is a problem with a teacher demonstrating minimum competence, it is best to abandon the formative procedure and instead, to adopt a specific plan of assistance that is followed by summative evaluations. Formative procedures are preferred for teachers who demonstrate, at the least, minimum competency.

One problem with any evaluation system is that of time. When there is not adequate time, the process has a tendency to become perfunctory. It is probable that teachers who have previously demonstrated competence may not need yearly summative evaluations. This is one of the main reasons that both formative and summative evaluation procedures are recommended—even competent teachers can benefit from a yearly growth plan.

One school system that uses both summative and formative processes evaluates most teachers summatively on a triennial basis. This plan is designed so that one-third of the teachers are evaluated each year. As a result, the number of yearly summative evaluations is small enough for the principal to conduct these evaluations on a comprehensive basis.

ELIMINATING CONFUSION

Figure 1-2 illustrates a frequent outcome of mixing formative and summative evaluation. How might some of the problems of mixing formative and summative evaluations be avoided? The following are some suggestions:

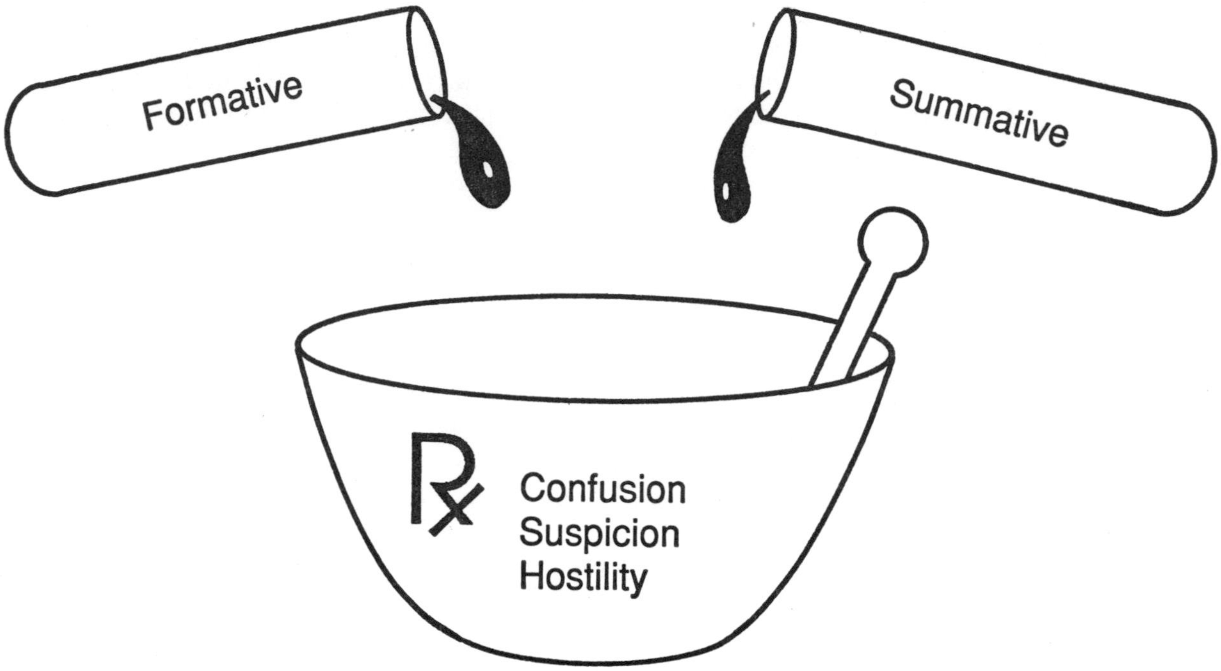

Figure 1-2 Mixing Purposes of Evaluation.

- Use two separate systems.
- Establish clear policies on the use of formative and summative evaluation.
- Notify teachers about when and why information will be gathered.
- Make a clear distinction in the personnel who use each procedure.
- Label each purpose with a distinct name.

Each of these suggested methods for avoiding "mixing" will be discussed.

Separate Systems

As previously stated, a frequent problem of evaluation is the attempt to accomplish the various purposes of evaluation in a single evaluative instrument. A frequent result is that no purpose is effectively served. Most research on evaluation supports a position that a single instrument cannot serve both summative and formative functions. There may be those who can effectively place all purposes of evaluation in a single instrument, but such evaluators are rare.

The use of two separate systems offers the possibility of a clear, relatively simple, and effective approach to evaluation. With a dual system, the formative evaluation can be used exclusively for growth. Peers can be trained to assist in the process. Of course, summative evaluation remains the responsibility of administration.

Summative evaluations could be made by different evaluators trained in summative procedures. The combinations of personnel who could conduct formative and summative evaluations are numerous, but peers should be involved in some part of the formative process. One of the most important rules of formative evaluation is that the information gathered has but one use—to guide growth. When the chips are down, there may be a tendency to use formative information to support a summative procedure, but doing so will quickly eliminate any chance for the formative procedure to produce a positive result.

Clear Policies

A clear and concise policy with regard to evaluation is desirable. In order for the teaching staff to "buy" into any evaluative process, they must know clearly when the growth process is in operation and when the rating process is in use. In other words, they must know the element of risk involved. Below is a policy statement used by one school system:

Administrative Evaluation

Generally, classroom observations are for the purpose of instructional improvement rather than administrative evaluation for continued employment. Classroom observations become administrative only when the principal makes a determination that, even with supervisory assistance, there is continuing unsatisfactory performance. The teacher is *notified in writing* when classroom observations are administrative in nature or when assessments are being made to determine recommendation for further employment. Specific performance expectations are communicated in writing when a plan of assistance or administrative review process begins, and the classroom observations are made by the principal or other administrators. (*Orange County Assessment For Professional Development*, Orange County Public Schools, Orange, Virginia 22960)

It is noteworthy that the teacher receives notice in writing when a status change is involved. This procedure lends a degree of security, because the teachers know that any information gathered prior to notification of a performance problem will not be used for summative purposes.

Notification of Purposes

When and why information is being collected should be made clear to the teaching staff. Communication is one of the most important aspects of an evaluation. Teachers cannot work in an insecure environment. There should be no hidden agendas, and any information collected should be used only for the purpose stated. Below is an example of a case which demonstrates the need to keep purposes clear and lines of communication open:

> A teacher filed a grievance with the administrator charged with the overall responsibility for the evaluation policy. The purpose of the grievance was to air the teacher's dissatisfaction with the school principal over not receiving proper recognition at the end of the year for work done as part of the formative evaluation process. Upon checking, it was found that the teacher completed most of the formative work. However, it was also discovered that the principal had concerns about certain aspects of the teacher's overall performance. As a result of these concerns, the principal had not been enthusiastic about advising the teacher how to recieve the financial recognition given to those teachers who demonstrated growth as part of the formative plan. (The recognition system involved a small incentive payment given for actively working toward success in a specific plan for growth.) The policy administrator's decision was that the teacher should be given further opportunity to receive additional formative evaluation and the sought-after recognition. The principal was advised to analyze overall performance concerns through the use of summative procedures.

The chief point of this example is that formative procedures must remain with the growth process and should *not* be used to make "status" decisions or responses. Conversely, when basic competence is a question, the teacher should be evaluated within the framework of the summative procedure. The teacher should know where he or she stands at all times.

It should be noted that the shift to the use of summative procedures will probably be required for only a few teachers. Even for these teachers, efforts to provide assistance should not cease. A key point is one of open communication. If status (tenure, job assignment, retention, etc.) is at stake, the teacher must be informed.

Different Personnel

The summative and formative purposes of evaluation can be kept separate if different personnel are used for each purpose. It is unreasonable to expect the principal to "blow the whistle" on marginal performance and to conduct the program of professional growth simultaneously. Such a procedure would also be counter-productive from the viewpoint of teacher morale. Credibility is difficult to achieve when the mode of operation is: "I'm here to help; however, if you need help, I will document." Using different personnel for each purpose of evaluation helps keep the purposes separated. Another problem which is relieved by involving a large number of personnel in evaluation is that of time. In traditional systems, the principal is usually assigned the duty of evaluation. In many schools, the simple logistics required for the principal to complete this task make positive results almost impossible

A Distinct Name

Growth and the measuring processes can be differentiated by giving each a distinct name. One suggestion is to designate the formative procedure as *assessment,* and the summative process as *evaluation.* This distinction will help in policy writing, in assigning tasks, and in the creation of forms, etc. Because of the previously discussed tendency to combine both types of evaluation into a single procedure, we did not use different names for these procedures in this chapter. In policy writing, however, using different terminology for these procedures is beneficial.

The following is a list of questions that may be helpful as a first step in devising a plan for evaluation which keeps growth and measuring procedures separated and staff involvement high:

1. What is the goal of evaluation?
2. Is there an evaluation policy which separates formative and summative evaluation?
3. Will all parties (evaluators and evaluatees) be involved in writing the evaluation policy?
4. Is there a plan to involve representatives of the teaching staff in identifying teacher characteristics to be evaluated?
5. Does the planning generated under Items 2, 3 and 4 complement the goal of evaluation?
6. What is the plan to communicate the goals of evaluation?

A MODEL FOR EVALUATION

A model of evaluation is show in Figure 1-3. In this model, the growth procedure and the accountability procedure are separated. Through the use of this model, a defensible checklist—or preferably a narrative, or a combination of the two—may

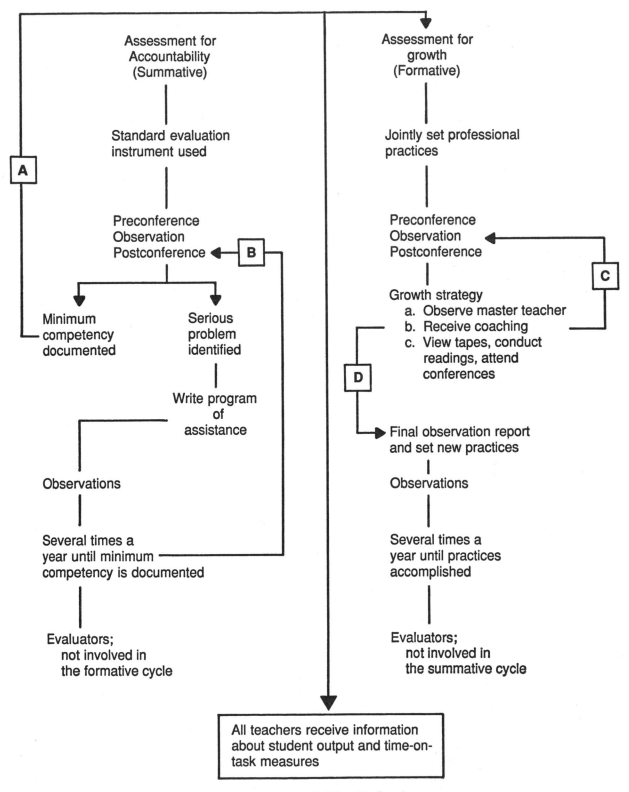

Figure 1-3 A Model for Evaluation.

be developed. This model will help those designing teacher evaluation to keep summative and formative procedures separate.

It can be noted from the evaluation model that there is a growth procedure (called assessment) and an accountability procedure (called evaluation). This model actually complements staff development as well as evaluation, for its goal is to have all memebers of the teaching staff working together at the assessment phase.

Note that those teachers evaluated summatively are moved to the growth procedure (A) as soon as minimum competency is documented. Those with identifiable problems are recycled (B) until minimum competency is identified or until they are finally placed on administrative review. The assessment cycle starts with setting professional practices; if a formative instrument is available, the goals are chosen from a list of desired competencies. The observation procedure and the setting of growth strategies proceed through cycle (C) one or more times until there is mutually agreed-upon final observation from which a growth report is completed.

One might ask, "If the assessment procedure is indeed formative, what is done with the growth report?" In the assessment procedure, the teacher decides. In some cases, the report is used to generate a motivational certificate; in others, the principal files the report in a growth packet kept separate for each teacher. The main concern is that this process have credibility with teachers. A report from the formative assessment process should not come to be used in a summative manner. The designers of evaluation should determine a response to the following questions. Of course, the answers should be based upon the unique circumstances of each school or school system.

1. Which teachers are to be evaluated for growth, and which for accountability? (For example, first-year teachers might be evaluated for accountability. Once minimum competency is documented, accountability evaluations may occur at less frequent intervals.)

2. What type of instrument is to be used for each kind of evaluation?

3. What will occur after minimum competency is established? (For example, is the teacher finished for the year, or is a change to the growth model desired? If so, what are cutoff dates for entering the growth program?)

4. What teacher characteristics are to be observed with each procedure? (For example, are there a few central skills—perhaps, basic skills—that are essential for the minimum competency? What are the other characteristics which lead to effective classroom practice for the growth model?)

5. What common information or feedback will be relayed to all teachers? (For example, in the model shown, all teachers receive student output information—i.e., test scores, learning goal accomplishments, and time-on-task analysis. Student output information and time-on-task analysis can be channeled into either process as appropriate.)

6. What kind of procedure will be utilized for those with identified problems, and what comprises a program of assistance?

MOTIVATION AND EVALUATION

Harrassment was mentioned in the title of this chapter; and in many instances when out-of-date evaluation procedures are used, teachers may tend to equate evaluation with harassment. Of course, the feeling of harassment is not consistent with good teacher motivation.

Ultimately, the primary purpose of evaluation must be to improve teaching. Unless teachers are motivated to achieve, little improvement will result. Therefore, any effort to devise an effective system of evaluation must take into account teacher motivation, which can be defined as feelings associated with the desire of the teacher to perform his or her job in an excellent manner.

Motivation is composed of a negative and positive aspect. Negative motivators are those aspects of the job which create dissatisfaction. Some negative motivators are criticism, low salary, lack of necessary equipment, and disapproval.

Positive motivators are those aspects of the job which create job satisfaction. Some positive motivators are automony, recognition, achievement, and responsibility. (See below.)

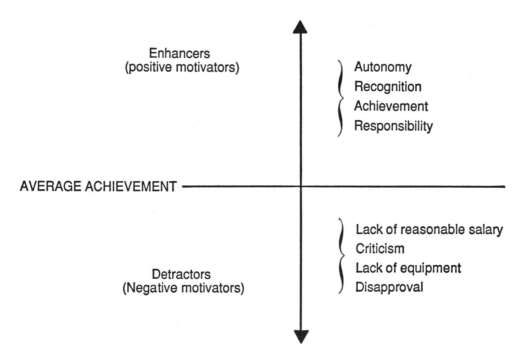

Note: the positive motivators will accelerate the desire to achieve. However, the negative motivators will detract from achievement if not reasonably meet.

Unless the function of both negative and positive motivators in understood, actions of the employer to motivate may, in fact, produce a result not desired. For example, the act of increasing salary (without attending to other motivators) will not of itself create positive motivation. Salary improvement may eliminate negative motivation. Improving salary is beneficial when a low salary scale is creating morale problems, but this act, which removes a negative motivator, does not by itself create additional motivation. It just creates a climate where positive motivation can succeed. In other words, some motivators only function to create problems if not reasonable met, but other motivators will create the desire to perform in a more excellent manner. (This section has been adapted from Herzberg; see bibliography.)

Improved performance is achieved by adding qualities that support positive motivators to the job. This theory of motivation is supported by a considerable body of research (see bibliography for suggested readings) and leads to some of the following assumptions:

1. The prospect of improving performance by increasing salary alone is not promising.
2. Improved performance is not likely to result from criticism; e.g., a classroom visitation where the faults in performance are identified.
3. Improved performance is not likely to result from the addition of teaching equipment. (Note, however, such actions may reduce dissatisfaction and facilitate the removal of "roadblocks.")
4. Improved performance is likely to result from actions which help the teaching staff gain a sense of autonomy, recognition, collegiality, achievement, and responsibility.

A program of evaluation can be used to address positive motivators, negative motivators, or both. Evaluation for growth is likely to contain more positive motivators than evaluation designed to ensure accountability. The motivational assumptions discussed above tend to add an additional dimension to the list of difficulties that arise when evaluations are "mixed," as was discussed earlier. To complement the need for motivation properly, an evaluation procedure should be designed to enrich work by providing positive motivators.

Consistent with motivation theory, an appropriate question might be, "What are some administrative procedures which enhance productive outcomes in the evaluation process?" The following suggestions merit some serious consideration:

1. Involve teachers in establishing the evaluation program.
2. Demonstrate a positive approach to evaluation—catch teachers doing good things.
3. Use criticism and negative input as a last resort and with the summative process.

4. Make evaluation a top priority in terms of time and resources.
5. Demonstrate commitment to the evaluation instrument or procedure by supporting regular in-service training.
6. Make sure that the evaluation process contains positive motivators.

Each of these suggestion for enhancing the evaluation process with teacher motivation will be discussed in the following pages.

Teacher Involvement

Efforts to promote teacher motivation through active involvement in the decision-making process produces mixed results at best. An expeditious review of survey results used to determine teacher perceptions of their involvement in decision making reveals that teachers tend to indicate a similar amount of involvement in schools with "high teacher input" as compared to those schools identified with "low teacher input." These results do not lead to the conclusion that teacher involvement should not be sought, but they do point to the fact that involvement alone will not make teachers feel involved. Some administrative actions designed to heighten teacher recognition of their involvement are the following:

1. Create high visibility in appointing teacher representatives.
2. Feature teachers involved in decision making in newsletters and other internal publications.
3. Publish summaries of minutes of committees and commissions with a listing of teacher representatives.
4. Conduct staff development meetings that explore the nature of involvement in decision making.
5. Give recognition to teachers who serve on input committees by giving them certificates of appreciation, personal letters of commendation, and recognition in staff meetings.
6. Create opportunities for teachers who are involved in committee work to report to school boards, parent-teacher organizations, the superintendent, etc.

To advocate staff development meetings in "involvement" may be viewed as curious, for it would appear as obvious that most educators understand the meaning of involvement. However, this is not the case. In fact, very few teachers have a clear perception of involvement in decision making. What administrator has not taken pride in the "fine work" of a committee composed mostly of teachers only to find that, when committee recommendations are adopted, some members of the teaching staff charge that teachers have "no input" in the decision-making process. This example serves to highlight the need for a better understanding of teacher involvement. It is also important that teachers review the perceptions of other players who have a stake in decision making and, of course, that these teachers have an understanding of input perimeters.

One reason often cited for ineffectiveness of teacher involvement is that teachers are involved so rarely that they don't know how to respond to serious opportunities. This may be true to some extent, but it only highlights the need of staff development in the involvement process. Through enhancing teacher perception of involvement, those astute enough to involve teachers will find that these teachers show increased motivation.

A Positive Approach

A positive approach to evaluation is a means of demonstrating a basic trust in teachers. It is knowing that more than ninety percent of the teaching staff will equal or exceed reasonable performance expectancies. About eight percent may need significant assistance. (The remaining two percent are discussed in Chapter 7.)

Being positive in evaluation involves a concept of teaching and teachers which embraces the view that there are identifiable variables for effective teaching. Being positive also requires believing that most teachers will make a sincere effort to adopt research-based practices if they are provided with assistance in the form of modeling, coaching, and feedback.

A positive approach may be enhanced by involving teachers extensively in the process of documenting the strengths of other teachers. They can also assist in designing the growth plan to utilize these strengths.

The most important element of the positive approach is for leadership to anticipate that growth will occur as a result of the evaluation program. The goal is for the professional climate of a school or school system to become one of growth. For this to occur, the evaluation program must become both growth promoting and nonthreatening for the overwhelming majority of teachers.

Criticism and Negative Input

Most administrators have attended an evaluation postconference where many positive attributes of teaching performance were stressed, but have noted that the conference seemed to deteriorate when a single critical assessment became its focus. Administrators who find that such conferences occur should question the continued use of the "strong points / weak points" approach.

If the characteristics of effective teaching are clearly defined and if anecdotal records are kept of each characteristic observed, it is usually sufficient simply to make no mention of characteristics that are not observed. Most teachers will seek to determine how they may demonstrate that which was not recorded. Assistance for the teacher may be provided at this point. If the teacher does not initiate the inquiry, the observer may initiate it by seeking clarification of the observation from the teacher or by making arrangements to revisit the classroom at a time the teacher is likely to use the characteristic. Because of possible deterioration of relationships, criticism and negative input should not be used until all else has failed.

Evaluation as a Top Priority

The program of evaluation defines teaching perhaps more than any written document which schools may develop. The procedures within the evaluation system also help to define the culture of the school and school system. The institutional perception of teachers as professional persons and as human beings is also reflected in the evaluation procedure. If evaluation is viewed from this important perspective, it is easy to understand why sufficient time and resources for its proper implementation become a must.

It is noteworthy that student learning is enhanced in schools where evaluation is stressed. Apparently, this positive effect of evaluation is true to some extent even if the evaluation procedures are poorly developed. Therefore, to place evaluation high on the agenda in terms of time and resources is critical for the promotion of student learning.

Commitment through In-service

In-service or staff development is a necessity if any program of evaluation is to be productive. Chapter 5 is devoted entirely to evaluation as a basis for staff development. To avoid redundancy, let us simply state that, when in-service is offered to the evaluators and evaluatees on a continuing basis, all involved become committed to the process. A tenet of management is the following: when management values a behavior or policy, the first step that management adopts is to make its value known. Most employees, professional and nonprofessional, seek to give competent service. Knowing what is important helps to give each member of an organization a share in the organizational vision.

Positive Motivators

In the previous discussion, it was stressed that some motivators will remove concerns which hamper work and that other movitators will create a desire to perform more effectively. Both kinds of motivation are useful, but it is advantageous to know how they differ. Once motivators are differentiated, assess to determine if negative motivators are the cause of problems by changing the agenda for improved performance. An assessment will also reveal if positive motivators are included in the evaluation procedure.

It is recognized that the use of the evaluation procedure as a motivational vehicle may appear unusual. Consider, however, that a purpose of evaluation is growth. Growth is enhanced if learners are motivated. Students are not the only learners in the school setting. It is true that evaluation is typically viewed by teachers as harassment or a nuisance, but change is advocated in evaluation procedures. Evaluation can become central to all efforts to improve teaching and learning, as is shown in Figure 1-4.

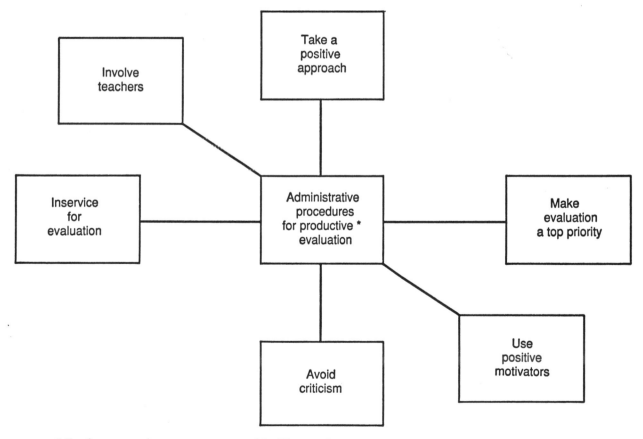

* Further procedures are suggested in Chapter 2.

Figure 1-4 Summary of Initial Evaluation Considerations.

SUMMARY

The main point of this chapter is that evaluation is much more than a simple summary of performance. Evaluation can enhance the following aspects of teaching and organizational life:

1. Support a plan for instructional improvement.
2. Satisfy the public's need for accountability.
3. Provide a structured plan for growth.
4. Give security to the teaching environment.
5. Provide motivation for teachers.
6. Define the practice of teaching.
7. Serve as the basis for staff development.

It is stressed that traditional once- or twice-a-year checklist evaluations tend to offer limited opportunity for the improvement of teaching. Teachers realize the inconsistency inherent in a procedure which is both formative and summative, and there is a very real possibility that they perceive this type of evaluation as a "necessary evil" or even as job harassment.

The following should be emphasized in the development of an effective evaluation system:

1. The formative and summative aspects of evaluation should be placed in two separate systems, or they should be incorporated into a single system in a manner that avoids mixing the two.
2. Teachers should be involved in designing the evaluation procedure and identifying teacher characteristics to be evaluated. (More is offered on "what is worth evaluating" in Chapter 2.)
3. Motivation of teachers should be recognized as a critical component of any program of teacher evaluation.
4. Evaluation should be placed among the very highest priorities of a school or school system, and resources of time and money should be devoted to the process.

Finally, there is a serious question about the transportability of evaluation systems. The intent of this book is to give the reader a conceptual background necessary to improve an existing evaluation system or devise a new system. A packaged system is not given. To include such a system almost ensures failure. It is believed that the most productive approach is to give the reader practical information that can be coordinated with local goals, and cultural and political parameters. The end result may then be an evaluative system which serves as a focus for an outstanding instructional program. Chapter 1 is viewed as the first step in a systematic effort to accomplish this task.

chapter 2

WHAT'S WORTH EVALUATING

During the last decade, there has been a tremendous amount of research about effective teaching practices. Rather than list all of the recommended research on effective teaching in this chapter, a method of utilizing available information will be explained. By using this chapter as a guide, it is anticipated that administrators and teachers will be able to organize local action research units to write summaries of desired teaching competencies. This local research can then become the basis for a locally developed teacher evaluation system.

As mentioned in Chapter 1, the exporting of a teacher evaluation system is difficult. A "prepackaged" system that is borrowed from another locality or imposed by the state offers little promise for improving instruction. This is caused by feelings of lack of ownership on the part of local staff and by the fact that an externally developed system cannot take local conditions into account.

The method of deciding "what's worth evaluating", which is treated in the following pages, will keep the process close to research-based teaching practice. The use of this method will also resolve the problem of ownership, for all decisions can be made consistent with local philosophy, needs, and in the local operational climate.

GETTING STARTED

There should be broad representation of those whom evaluations will affect in any group engaged in deciding what is worth evaluating. The importance of teacher involvement was discussed in Chapter 1, but the involvement of the principal is often overlooked. Evaluation has a primary impact upon the principal as well as the teacher. The principal has a significant stake in the evaluation process, because he or she must evaluate as a primary job responsibility. The principal must also maintain "esprit de corps," project competence, and ensure instructional program improvements. All these factors relate to the evaluation procedure. If the evaluation procedure is antiquated, inadequate, and unproductive, the principal automatically loses credibility in any attempt to evaluate.

To be consistent with the above statements, no evaluation system should be devised or upgraded without the heavy involvement of teachers and principal, who should be organized into research units to determine what teacher competencies will be evaluated. Figure 2-1 illustrates steps for structuring local research units.

Composition of Research Units

The composition of the research units has a long-range effect upon the success of the evaluation system. The composition should be as inclusive as possible. Teachers and principals must be members of these units, and membership for school board members, patrons, and central office staff should also be considered. It is advantageous to create public interest in the revision of the evaluation process, since involvement engenders feelings of ownership. There is no one best method for the composition or use of local research units. Varied plans may produce comparable, favorable results. Within these units, a sequence of work should be followed that will lead to the identification of between eight and twelve competencies. The competencies should be specifically defined with performance indicators. This is the task of the secondary units.

Identifying Competencies Desired

A review of research about proven teaching practices will be helpful in deciding which teaching practices to evaluate. Consult the bibliography for a starting point. A list of teaching competencies chosen by others is offered later in this chapter and in Appendix 1. These lists will provide material for ideas and for comparison. A choice of six to eight competencies is probably a manageable number for evaluation. However, if evaluation is to become a part of staff development, you may wish to select more competencies (twelve to seventeen) to evaluate in a multiyear effort.

The Written Narrative and Performance Indicators

Performance indicators must be identified for each competency. It is advisable to develop a written summary of each competency, and then to draw from this summary a list of performance indicators. The written summary can be used when future questions arise about the meaning of a performance indicator. Finally, an editing committee is needed. The responsibility of this committee is proper grammar, consistent writing sytle, and format.

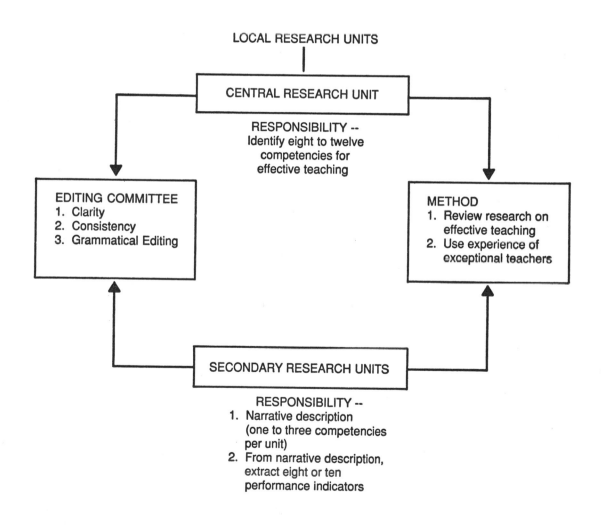

Figure 2-1 Constructing an Evaluation System.

THE RESPONSIBILITIES OF LOCAL RESEARCH UNITS

Figure 2-2 is a structure for planning the work of local research units. This diagram is similar to Figure 2-1 except that a policy committee has been added. Its function is to recommend the "rules" of evaluation.

The desired teacher competencies may be identified by an initial research unit. Then, secondary research units may be assigned one or two competencies each. The responsibilities of each unit should be to make a careful survey of pertinent research, interview experienced teachers, and write a narrative summary

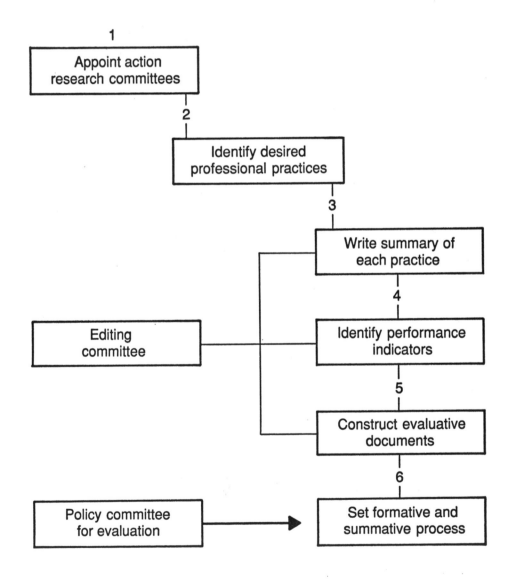

Figure 2-2 Six Steps to Designing the Evaluative Instrument.

of the teacher actions which could be observed in the classroom. From the narrative summary, a list of eight or ten performance indicators should be listed.

EXAMPLES OF PROFESSIONAL PRACTICES

Two examples are given—*evaluating students* and *classroom management*. After a summary of each of these teacher competencies, a list of performance indicators is given. These examples can be used as models for the work of local research units.

Example One—Evaluating Students

An extremely important aspect of teaching is the evaluation of students. Evaluation is such a basic part of teaching that it is commonly believed to be the end product—a measure for student performance rather than for the teaching process. However, the evaluation procedures used by a teacher reveal more about the classroom than any other index except that of classroom observation. Figure 2-3 illustrates the minimum components of student evaluation.

Instructional objectives form the yardstick for viewing a teacher's grasp of the importance of careful evaluation. The teacher's ability to make evaluation a vital component of instruction rather than an adjunct activity is readily determined by looking at the fusing of instructional objectives with preassessment, formative sampling, and summative assessment. All these components form the basis for sound evaluation. (See Figure 2-4.)

Clearly articulated instructional objectives state what is to be learned and what the students will be able to do as a result of instruction. Each component of evaluation and all teaching strategies must relate to the stated objectives. The concern is for evaluation to measure what was taught, and that the material taught and the instructional methodology relate to stated objectives. An example of failure to coordinate all phases of evaluation to the instructional objectives and to link assessment to instructional methodology follows:

> Mr. Jones's instructional objective was stated as follows: "Students shall demonstrate an understanding of the causes of the Civil War." As instruction proceeded, students were assigned the basic reading material, work groups were formed, and two role-playing groups were established—one each for North and South. A third group formed discussed geographical facts with student-made maps. Some students worked on group assignments, while those who had shown need for intensive instruction received Mr. Jones's special attention.

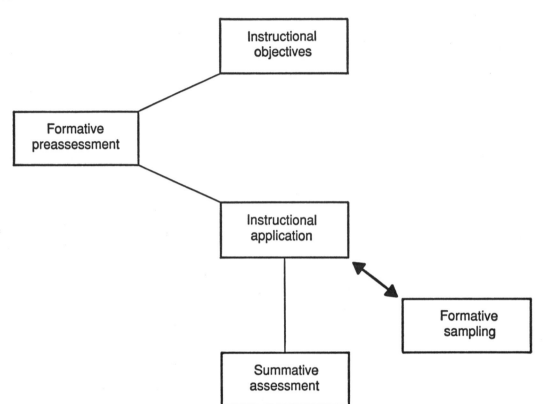

Figure 2-3 Minimum Components of Student Evaluation.

Finally, it was examination time. The examination was composed of true/false and multiple-choice questions that were machine-scored. Four students failed; three students made A's; and the remaining students received grades evenly distributed among B, C, and D.

It can be observed in the above example that several components of effective student evaluation were missing from an instructional process which incorporated some diverse learning activities. For example, the instructional objective did not state what the students would be able to do as a result of instruction. How were the students to "demonstrate an understanding"? There appears to have been no preassessment or formative sampling, and the final examination tested simple recall, which could have been learned effectively by spending the learning time with basic reading material. There were no provisions for reteaching.

Clearly, the student evaluation procedure used by Mr. Jones did not achieve the desired coordination of objectives with instructional methodology, for the summative evaluation tested only simple recall. In this environment, the students soon learn that only the memorizing of facts is important and that the rest is "fun and games." This leads to motivational problems, since students view the other learning activities, such as group work, as immaterial. A rule to remember is the

The Assessment Instrument

Teacher Competency or Professional Practice: Evaluating Students

Directions: The observer will describe in writing exactly what was observed that demonstrates each of the performance indicators. Absence of a written description for any indicator means that the observer did not observe performance thought to demonstrate the indicator during the observation period.

Description: Student evaluation is a vital part of the teaching process. Included is preassessment, formative sampling, and testing for grades (summative). A student evaluation plan must be tied to the learning objectives, and these must state student performance expected.

The following performance indicators can be observed when an effective plan of student evaluation is in place:

1. Objectives for instruction are clearly stated.
2. Student expectancies are included as part of the objectives.
3. Basic instruction and enrichment relate to the instructional objectives.
4. Preassessment is made prior to the beginning of instruction.
5. Formative sampling techniques are used.
6. Summative tests relate to stated objectives.
7. Summative tests relate to instructional delivery and methodology.
8. A plan for reteaching is observed.
9. Formative sampling and instruction are used only as a gauge for instructional decisions.
10. Provisions are made for testing, at the least, recall, comprehension, and application.

Figure 2-4

following one: *students tend to learn that which is important from the communication sent by the teacher's evaluation methods.* Therefore, all components of student evaluation must be present.

Another teaching practice which creates problems in relating testing to objectives is that of assigning grades to formative activities. When this procedure is observed, it is usually an indication that the teacher is uncomfortable with student control and motivation. When quizzes, group participation, and homework are graded and averaged as part of the final grade, then the formative activities are being used as disciplinary tools! These are "low effort," coercive attempts to motivate by using threats. This mixing of formative and summative procedures in student evaluation has the same negative effect for student evaluation as in teacher evaluation. The end result is often a hostile and threatening environment.

Preassessment. This component of student evaluation is used to determine students' knowledge about the learning objectives prior to the beginning of instruction. Preassessment includes a sampling of requisite skills, as well as the instructional material to be learned. The result of preassessment is to determine those in need of significant basic instruction, as well as those who need very little basic instruction prior to enrichment or extension activities.

It can never be assumed that all students in a class will learn the same material, presented in the same manner, at the same time. Most teachers and administrators are vividly aware of this fact, but accommodating different levels and different methods of instruction simultaneously takes skill and effort. Preassessment is viewed as the first clue in the effort to meet the differing needs of students.

Formative Sampling. The use of formative sampling is a further dimension to examine in determining teacher competence in the evaluative aspect of instruction. Formative sampling may be conducted in a number of ways. These include questioning techniques, where student understanding is sampled by having those who can correctly answer give hand signals. This method of sampling provides the teacher with information relative to the progress of instruction and assists in identifying those in need of additional instruction. Other sampling techniques include ungraded quizzes, practice assignments, and homework.

Summative Assessment. This method is designed to determine what has been learned. It is used to make "status" decisions about students, such as grades, promotions, and reteaching recommendations. A large number of highly competent teachers use a structured program of reteaching for students who fail to pass a summative test. Adherents of Bloom's mastery learning concepts believe that most students can learn almost any subject matter, and that, to a greater extent, learning is a product of time than of ability. Those who ascribe to this philosophy must devise a "reteach" structure.

A Final Word on Student Evaluation. Another insight into teaching competence which can be observed through student evaluation is the required depth of student knowledge. Students usually forget items learned for simple recall shortly after the summative test. It is true that some basic facts must be learned by rote memory, but instruction should not shop here. As soon as the requisite facts are learned, instruction should proceed to what is known as the "higher levels" of learning. This requires students to comprehend what was learned and to apply the learning to new situations. Many students can engage in more advanced learning activities, such as analysis and synthesis. However, recall, comprehension, and application are essential if long-term learning is to be enhanced. Tests should be devised to require responses from all three areas. Remember, students learn what is important from what is tested.

Example Two—Classroom Management

Classroom management incorporates the teacher's ability to "guide" the enterprise of learning. Teaching, like any professional endeavor or business organization, has certain organizational techniques which promote the task to be accomplished.

From the managerial perspective, a well-managed classroom might be compared with a modern dentist's office. Transition from the waiting room to the operatory is accomplished in a manner to avoid wasting the dentist's time. An assistant has placed the appropriate tools in a prescribed order, and previous records are open, ready for the doctor to review. Preliminary work is accomplished by a technician. When his or her work is completed, the dentist leaves the operatory. The patient's exit procedures are the responsibility of others. During the entire process, the impression is one of organization to utilize a precious commodity—*time*. Time is also the crux of classroom management. The teacher's time must be utilized in interacting with students, and the student time must be engaged in learning. (See Figure 2-5).

Transitions. One of the most notable characteristics of a well-managed classroom is a transition activity to initiate learning. Beginning transitions are activities which allow students to begin work at different times as they enter the classroom. These activities may include the following: students select a line from the literary assignment for the day and write a paragraph about what it might mean; students create a few test questions from yesterday's lesson. This work could be collected to augment any portion of a planned review. The teacher could randomly select a few of the test questions and ask "Who can answer this question?" Of course, the contributor's name should be given. Beginning transition activities can increase class participation and reduce lost time while students are entering the classroom and getting settled for work.

Transitions are also important when the class activities are being changed. For example, when a teacher is changing the class activity from direct instruction to project work, time and class control may be lost as students put away note pads and get project materials. All transitions should be planned so that time is saved, and control is maintained.

Expectancies. A classroom can be adequately managed only if there is

Assessment Instrument

Teacher Competency: Classroom Management

Directions: The observer will describe in writing exactly what was observed that demonstrated each of the performance indicators. Absence of a written description for any indicator means that the observer did not observe performance thought to demonstrate the indicator during the observation period.

Description: Classroom management techniques are necessary to create a learning environment where time and resources are used effectively. A well-managed classroom has organized routines for accomplishing the necessary management functions, and interruptions are reduced. Planning for a well-managed classroom can be observed by fulfillment of the following performance indicators:

1. Transition activities are organized to reduce the loss of time.
2. High expectancies for student behavior are observed.
3. Routines for essential management activities are set.
4. Room arrangement complements learning.
5. The teacher moves about the classroom to enhance learning.
6. The teacher constantly "scopes" the classroom.
7. Expected behaviors are practiced.
8. At least ____% of learning time is utilized.
9. Direct instruction is utilized for at least ____% of on-task-time.
10. Change of pace is utilized to keep student motivation high.

Figure 2-5

clearly articulated expectancies for student behavior. Some of the most essential expectancies are those relative to use of student time. Procedures must be set for simple tasks such as getting supplies, sharpening pencils, attending rest room, etc. There is also an expectancy regarding respect for others and the success of each learner. Each student is expected to be on-task.

Room Arrangement. Attention to room arrangement is a component of the well-managed classroom. Lighting, displays that relate to the learning objectives, and student seating should receive attention. Each of these "physical" components is important for learning. A burned-out light or an inhibiting glare from the sun should not be tolerated. Bulletin boards are often viewed as "something to cover." However, they are not in the classroom to give the teacher experience in cutting and pasting. Bulletin boards should enhance the impression that the classroom is a place of planned purpose. Student seating must allow the teacher to circulate to every part of the class. Finally, all students must be able to see and hear adequately.

Teacher Movement. A critical management technique is teacher movement. Classrooms where the teacher sits at the desk are not as productive as classrooms where the teacher circulates. Circulating in the classroom is a class control mechanism. A teacher may anticipate student inattentiveness and simply move close to the problem. The bodily presence of the teacher may correct the potential probelm without taking the entire class off-task while the student is being corrected.

Scoping the Classroom. Teacher movement and other management strategies are dependent upon the teacher's ability to "scope" the classroom. Scoping involves doing two things at once—the task at hand plus viewing the classroom for any sign of off-task behavior. A common problem in classroom management is encountered when the teacher becomes engrossed with working in one area of the classroom and loses cognizance of what else is occurring. Scoping the classroom involves positioning the body so as to see most of the classroom at all times. It also involves constant movement to keep the total classroom in view.

Practicing Behaviors. Students cannot be expected to exhibit behavior patterns which complement good classroom management unless the expected behaviors are practiced. This applies equally to elementary and secondary teachers. Practice is actually coaching for effective classroom management. Practice is conducted in a number of ways consistent with student maturity level.

The goal of practice is that students learn to make rapid transitions. Examples of activities which need attention are entering the room, exiting the room, getting materials, forming into groups, sharpening pencils, and asking questions. All of these activities are practiced early in the school year and should become routines which operate smoothly thereafter.

Time-on-Task. One significant test for classroom management is a time-on-task measure. Time-on-task measures are used to determine the actual utilization of class time.

Measures of classroom time can help determine how many students are on-task as a percent of the time available. An observer divides the class period into segments of two to four minutes. During each segment, the classroom is scanned in order to determine: (1) students on-task; (2) students off-task; and (3) type of instruction (direct or indirect). The type of instruction is included, because more learning takes place when the students are interacting directly with the teacher. An assessment of time-on-task might be accomplished with a standard form. Each school or school system will need to decide the expectancy relative to what percent of the available class time should be on-task and what percent of time-on-task should involve direct instruction.

As observers gain expertise in using time-on-task measures, student success measures might be added. When students are experiencing a relatively high rate of success, learning is enhanced. An excellent source for those beginning to consider time-on-task measurement is a short publication available from the Northwest Regional Educational Laboratory (*How to Increase Learning Time*, by Hiscor, Branerman, and Exions, 300 S.W. South Avenue, Portland, Oregon 97204). A model observation instrument may be found in this publication.

Change of Pace. A very effective management tool is change of pace. It is utilized to keep the students interested and to make the classroom an exciting and dynamic place. The change of pace is most effective when students begin to get restless or to engage in off-task behavior. A sensitive teacher can tell when the classroom atmosphere becomes "dead." This is the time for a change of pace. It is true that a change of pace may cause the teacher to abandon temporarily the first-choice learning activity, but the result is that the classroom atmosphere becomes enlivened, and student attention is recaptured. The first-choice activity can be resumed after the learners have regained enthusiasm or have been "awakened" by the change of pace.

CONSIDERATIONS FOR EVALUATION

The Importance of Narrative Summary

It can be observed that performance indicators may give rise to many different interpretations. For example, Indicator 4 (Figure 2-5) "Room Arrangement Complements Learning," could be interpreted to mean that the student seats are connected to the floor—a prevalent practice two or three generations ago. With the written summary however, all observers would know that using this indicator means to observe for proper lighting, pertinent bulletin boards, a seating arrangement which allows the teacher to circulate, and to observe whether or not the students can see and hear adequately.

The written narrative for each professional practice should be available for each observer and each teacher. Of course, this becomes the document from which the professional practices are originally derived.

Observing the Professional Practices

In the process of identifying professional practices, several questions will arise. Some of these questions are listed and discussed as follows:

1. How can an observer properly observe ten or twelve professional practices and more than one hundred performance practices?

2. How can summative and formative instruments be constructed from the procedure advocated in this chapter?

Figure 2-6 demonstrates a four-year cycle of teacher assessment. Summative evaluation is anticipated at least once in the four-year cycle. The framers of the professional practices will be able to identify certain performance indicators which should be demonstrated with frequency. These indicators are compiled in a separate summary instrument and observed summatively. Additional work with time-on-task instruments and measures of student performance might also receive attention during the summative process. Remember, the summative evaluation can be conducted concurrently with the formative assessment, but the two processes have different purposes and should be kept separate.

Measure of Output or Student Performance

There is a growing consensus that any evaluation system which is to improve teaching must contain measures of student results. Those who do not fully subscribe to this view contend that the teaching profession is similar to the medical profession in that practitioners owe their clients "best practice," but cannot guarantee results. Advocates of results retort that, even though best practice is appropriate, there are some practitioners in both professions who have more success than others. Moreover, they feel that expectancies based upon the performance of the most successful are in order, considering the critical nature of both professions.

Conceding that measures of student performance are important, the problem arises about how this performance can be accurately measured. There is also the problem of how to measure student results without transforming a formative procedure into a summative one. With all the interest in student results, some answers to these and other concerns should emerge in the near future. In the meantime, a look at student results might be directed by the teacher. This way the teacher could forecast student results when setting learning objectives. The teacher may choose to use criterion reference tests, but should also consider the use of standardized tests.

With the states becoming more prescriptive than in the past, there may be a period of reliance on standardized tests to measure student results. There are several reasons why standardized tests are not appropriate for this purpose, but

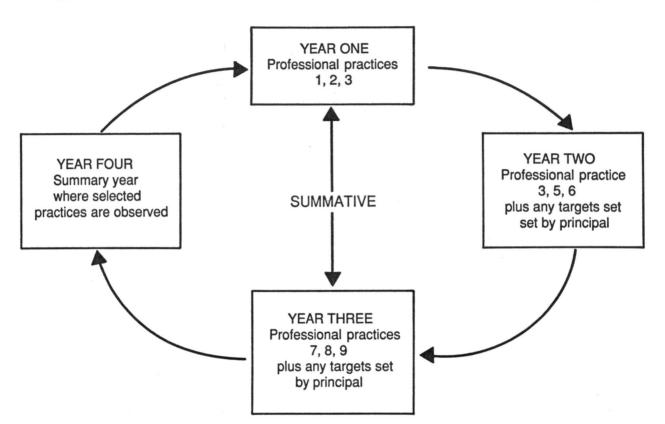

Figure 2-6 Four-year Cycle of Teacher Assessment.

pedagogical propriety and political expediency are not often cohorts. For this reason, administrators and teachers should experiment with ways to measure student performance and work while maintaining the growth component of evaluation, which can exist only in an atmosphere of mutual trust and respect.

CONSTRUCTING A SUMMATIVE INSTRUMENT

After deciding the appropriate professional practices and performance indicators, the question arises about how to accommodate the formative and the summative needs of evaluation. Figure 2-7 demonstrates the structure of an evaluation system with separate formative and summative procedures. The formative process can now

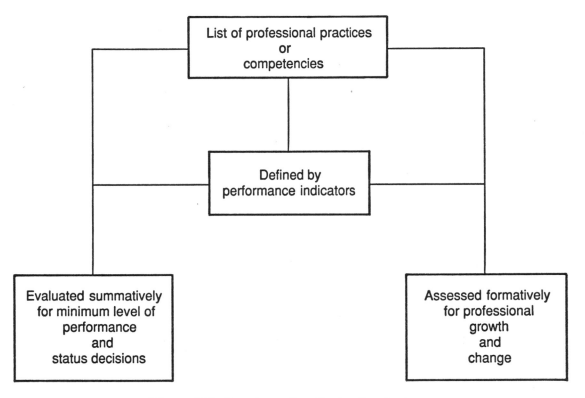

Figure 2-7 Structure of an Evaluation System.

utilize all information collected as a growth instrument. The summative procedure requires some additional thought.

As mentioned earlier, summative evaluation will probably be the domain of the school principal. The primary concern of summative evaluation should be minimum competency. Why minimum? Because summative evaluation is used mainly for ensuring a level of performance necessary to continue the contractual relationship. After minimum competency is documented, further assessment can be concerned with formative assistance.

In the summative mode, there is possibly one other activity for the principal. This is to help the teacher identify any performance indicator or any other characteristics that need attention. This purpose could be accomplished by setting an occasional job target. After identifying the purpose of the summative instrument, the main question becomes, *"How can a summative instrument be developed?"* A summative instrument can be developed by carefully reviewing the professional practices, and by identifying those thought to be essential for the maintenance of a minimum level of teaching performance. From this list, a summative list can be created.

Once the minimum level of performance has been established, there is one other needed addition. This is the nonperformance aspects of teacher competence, which may include some of the following:

1. Ability to work with other staff members
2. Ability to adhere to reasonable organizational expectancies, such as involvement in student extracurricular activities and punctuality
3. Support for school board policies
4. The ability to disagree in a nondestructive manner
5. A commitment to utilize professional opportunities, such as attending in-service meetings

There are other nonperformance characteristics which could be identified as necessary for productive relationships. Once these have been identified, the content of the summative instrument may be completed.

Finally, the summative instrument should contain space for the evaluator to describe precisely any area of needed improvement, as well as exact expectancies relative to anticipated improvement. It will be observed from reading Chapter 7 that checklists alone are often not adquate if the summative procedure becomes a subject of legal scrutiny.

Evaluating Summatively

The summative evaluation should be conducted every three or four years. Of course, first-year teachers and teachers in the process of obtaining tenure or continuing contract may need additional summative attention. If the summative evaluations are conducted on a periodic basis, policy should allow the principal to invoke the summative process at other times if there is an observed need.

The summative evaluation may proceed simultaneously with formative processes if different evaluators are used. If the principal is the summative evaluator, as has been suggested, he or she can easily conduct an evaluation for minimum competency without disturbing the work of peer evaluators.

Successful summative evaluation can be conducted only if the teacher clearly understands when the summative process begins and ends. There must also be clear understanding of the difference between summative and formative processes.

As a review, a summative evaluation is used to ensure accountability and minimum competency. The summative evaluation is nearly always tied to "status" decisions about the teacher, such as tenure, salary, placement, etc. If a formative procedure is used to make summative decisions, this usually causes the formative process to become summative and to lose any value it might have for enhancing growth.

THE QUESTION OF GENERIC OR CONTENT

In constructing an evaluation system, the question of whether or not the content area should be addressed is likely to arise. Those reluctant to participate in the change process with an effective program of evaluation may make the contention that the designed evaluation doesn't apply to their specific fields.

While content-specific assessment is important, by its very nature, its diversity poses a problem of great magnitude. How could a school or school system possibly address content-area assessment from the recognition of numbers up through calculus?

There are specific strategies which will help address the "content-area" concern. However, it is questionable to attempt to incorporate this area into an evaluation system. Consider the following:

1. How often does a serious problem arise with teacher knowledge of subject matter?
2. What other nonevaluative efforts are available to support content-specific development?

In response to the first question, it is unusual for a principal to encounter a teacher who has difficulty because of his or her lack of knowledge about the subject or subjects taught. This view is at odds with popular opinion. In fact, much of the thrust for educational reform came from a deep-seated belief that many teachers did not "know enough to teach."

Despite all the public clamor, this question can be settled by making an informal survey of a few building-level administrators within your immediate area. It is doubtful that these administrators will identify more than a handful of content deficient teachers from among several hundred. It is our contention that specific individualized programs should be developed for these teachers. It does not seem practical to "foul up" a good evaluation system by trying to reach them indirectly.

In answer to the second question, some of the following procedures (if not all) may be developed if they are not presently being implemented:

1. Required subject-area in-service
2. Classroom visits by subject-area specialist
3. Required basic content for each grade and secondary course
4. Minimum student competencies for the basic subjects
5. Interdepartmental peer visiting and meetings
6. University extension courses for specific subjects, such as teaching reading and math for the middle grades, etc.

Through these means, content concerns may be satisfactorily addressed. It is more appropriate to focus on the practice or the pedagogical aspects of teaching. Again, an informal survey of building principals will reveal many more concerns about classroom performance in such areas as student evaluation, classroom management, lesson plans, etc. These "generic" teaching practices are universal to teaching in all subject areas and grade levels.

It is through the identifying of "generic" teaching practices which are supported by a research base that the most improvement in teaching may be expected. Having local study committees (action research units) begin to focus on generic teaching practices creates the impetus for an excellent teacher evaluation system, and the entire professional climate of a school or school system can be changed to one of collegiality and growth. In the following pages, representative generic teaching practices that have been identified by others are discussed.

EXAMPLES OF PROFESSIONAL PRACTICES

Example One

In a study of evaluation instruments of national scope, Johnson and Orso* surveyed evaluation instruments used in large school systems from forty-eight states. The criteria for evaluations which were identified were placed under five broad categories: instruction, classroom management, professional responsibilities, personal characteristics, and interpersonal relations. Criteria which were selected by more than fifty percent of the school systems responding were the following:

Learning

1. Employs a variety of instructional media and instructional techniques
2. Implements the district instructional goals and objectives
3. Provides attention to individual differences
4. Evaluates students effectively and fairly on a regular basis
5. Shows written evidence of preparation for classes
6. Is knowledgeable of subject matter being taught
7. Reviews test results with students
8. Motivates students

---

* Nancy C. Johnson and J. Kenneth Orso, *"Teacher Evaluation Criteria," Spectrum: Journal of Research and Information,* Vol. 4, No. 3, Arlington, Virginia: Educational Research Service, Inc., Summer 1986.

Classroom Management

1. Establishes an environment conducive to learning
2. Disciplines in a fair manner
3. Provides a safe and orderly classroom

Professional Responsibilities

1. Participates in professional development activities, such as workshops, courses, and other school visits, etc.
2. Participates in school management and shares responsibility for the total school program
3. Completes reports accurately and submits them on time
4. Shows interest in improving skills
5. Observes school policies and procedures
6. Seeks information to become better informed about changes in education

Personal Characteristics

1. Uses clear speech
2. Exhibits neat, attractive (professional) personal appearance

Interpersonal Relations

1. Establishes positive relationship with students, parents, and the community

Note that the need for performance indicators is apparent. For example, how does one evaluate "shows interest" or "seeks information" without performance indicators of actions a teacher might take that demonstrates showing interest or seeking information.

Example Two

The teachers and administrators of the Orange County Public Schools* identified the following professional practices:

* *Assessments for Professional Development,* Orange County Public Schools, Orange, Virginia, July 1986.

1. Classroom routines
2. Essential techniques of instruction
3. Provisions for individual learning
4. Lesson plans and objectives for learning
5. Evaluation of student progress
6. Critical thinking and problem solving
7. Teacher-student rapport
8. Student motivation
9. Management of student behavior
10. Student participation in learning activities
11. Reports and routine duties
12. School and community relations

As part of the Orange County model, performance indicators are provided for each professional practice, and certain of the performance indicators which are believed to be critical for excellent teaching are combined to form an instrument used by principals as part of the summative process. The formative program (assessment) in Orange County is operated by peer observers.

Teachers complete three professional practices each year. After all professional practices are completed, the fifth year, which is the cycle completion year, is spent working with the summary performance indicator. The peer evaluators observe a number of these for frequency of use. After a cycle is completed, the teacher begins a new cycle.

Example Three

The Virginia Beginning Teacher Assistance Program (BTAP)* is a program adopted by the Virginia State Board of Education to "assist new teachers" by requiring that each teacher entering the profession demonstrate certain competencies. The assistance component is provided through fourteen assistance sessions—one session for each competency. Each session is composed of competency definition, background knowledge, and practice activities. The competencies are as follows:

1. Academic learning time
2. Student accountability
3. Clarity of lesson structure

* *Beginning Teacher Assistance Program*, Commonwealth of Virginia, Department of Education, Richmond, Virginia, 1986.

4. Individual differences
5. Evaluation
6. Consistent rules
7. Affective climate
8. Learner's self-concept
9. Meaningful learning
10. Planning
11. Questioning skills
12. Reinforcement
13. Close supervision
14. Awareness

The Virginia program shows considerable promise as the basis for an outstanding formative initiative. Political constraints presently require a mixture from a formative and summative agenda. The summative aspect is that state evaluators must document a beginning teacher's ability to demonstrate the competencies, or the teacher is refused a teaching certificate after the initial two-year certificate expires.

These few examples taken from local, state, and national sources modestly demonstrate the vast array of information available for those who wish to upgrade or initiate a new system of teacher evaluation. (Another example given in the Appendix follows the recommended structure very closely.) Identifying competencies for effective teaching can be accomplished by any school or school system. Carefully refining the definition of each competency to allow for objective assessment is time consuming, but with effort, this activity can build ownership and support a school-wide emphasis on effective teaching. (The six steps for designing an evaluative instrument were outlined in Figure 2-2.)

SUMMARY

Developing or upgrading a teacher evaluation system can be accomplished in a systematic manner. It is important to be certain that those affected most by the teacher evaluation system are involved. These are the teachers and the principal. The latest research on effective teaching practices should be incorporated into the evaluation system. A suggested way to accomplish this is through the utilization of local research units. A primary unit is suggested for identifying the desired teaching practices; and secondary research units are suggested for writing a narrative description of each professional practice and extracting appropriate performance indicators.

Generic teaching practices are suggested as appropriate content for evaluation system. There are other nonevaluative means to work with the "content-specific" needs of teachers. Most problems encountered regarding teacher competence arise from pedagogical deficiencies rather than from a lack of knowledge about subject matter.

There is concern in some quarters that the movement to identify teaching practices and performance indicators may lead to a prescriptive, stifling kind of teaching which omits the "art" of teaching. This need not be of concern, as the most creative teachers will be the first to find many novel ways to demonstrate effective teaching practice.

This chapter concludes with a review of some teacher competencies from national, state, and local sources. Those who wish to upgrade an existing system of evaluation or construct an entirely new system can use the information within this chapter and from the bibliography as an excellent starting point for creating an outstanding system of teacher evaluation. The next chapter will explain how a school or school system may train evaluators, and how an evaluation instrument can be used as a basis for staff development.

chapter 3

PEERS AS EVALUATORS

An effective teacher evaluation process is likely to utilize the assistance of peers. The principal's time is usually wholly taken up by his or her involvement in summative evaluations. Others, such as assistant principals and supervisors, do not have sufficient time to do an adequate job with formative evaluations. The need for formative evaluations and an emphasis on instructional improvement can be met with peer assistance.

The use of peers as evaluators can help to transform the evaluation process into a school improvement procedure. Peer evaluators can become involved in identifying competent teaching. Through utilization of peers, the possibility of staff ownership of the evaluation system is enhanced. There is increased morale, collegiality, and communication.

An outstanding side benefit occurs as peer observers visit classrooms. The peers also learn! (The use of the term, "observers," is intentional, for it is probably more accurate than the term, evaluators. Both terms, however, are used interchangeably.) The ambience of an entire school can be changed with peer observers. An appropriate question might be, "If all this is true—then why haven't peers been used all along?" The answer lies in the previous lack of a sound knowledge base for formative evaluation, tradition, outmoded beliefs, and lack of an operational model. This chapter is designed to dispel some of the reasons for reluctance to utilize peers, and to provide information about building an operational model that utilizes peer observers.

PEERS AS FORMATIVE ASSESSORS

Additional Observations Possible

Peer observers can help the formative evaluation program gain the needed factors of trust and collegiality. Through the vastly improved contacts that become possible with other significant adults/teachers, the improvement of instruction becomes the primary point of focus.

With the traditional teacher evaluative model, the teacher meets with the principal once or even twice a year to discuss classroom performance. With a formative evaluation model which uses peer obervers, every teacher can have at least six formative evaluations. Of course, these evaluations are in addition to any summative program the school retains. For demonstration purposes, Figure 3-1 is used to illustrate a program of formative evaluation which uses peers in a school with twenty teachers. Notice the large number (120) of formative evaluations which are possible. There are roadblocks for peer observers, and these will be discussed in the following pages. The extra effort required to solve these roadblocks is warranted, for achieving this recommended number of evaluations can, in fact, change the school climate for the better.

Trust of Colleagues

Trust is a very significant element in the growth process—particularly if growth is to occur with the assistance of another person. Fear of negative judgments on the part of the teacher has prevented those in authority from being effective in helping teachers to improve. From research it is assumed that more than three-fourths of the teachers believe themselves to be better than average in teaching ability.

Having someone in authority to identify a weakness in performance is somewhat traumatic. Peers can observe in an environment free of much of the fear that normally surrounds evaluation. Of course, this is true if peers are used only in the formative process as recommended.

Noted among the teaching staff during the last few years is a trend for teachers to accord each other high esteem and to regard colleagues as persons of high value. This trend has probably become stronger as external prestige of teachers has declined and the status of teachers in society has diminished. Regardless of the source of this teacher cohesiveness, it makes the climate for peer observers more acceptable than it was in the past.

The peer observer is viewed as a colleague who will help in a nonthreatening manner. Trust is a very significant element in the growth process—particularly if growth is to occur with the assistance of another person. This is the chief reason

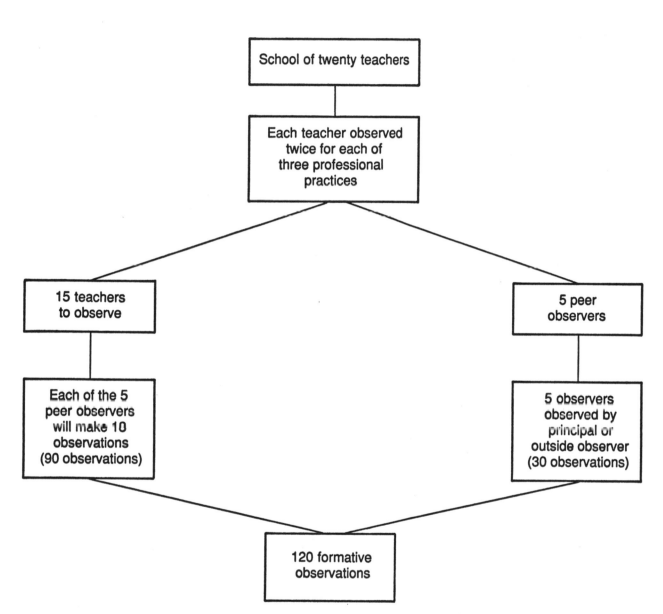

Figure 3-1 A Sample Program of Formative Evaluation.

why peers must be involved only in formative evaluation. Many who presently serve in administrative, supervisory, and teaching positions do not fully understand the difference in summative and formative evaluation. For this reason, the practice of using peer observers will meet resistance unless care is taken. Teacher involvement in creating the evaluation system must be incorporated into an overall plan, as was suggested in Chapter 2. For peers to experience this trust, three actions must be avoided:

1. Don't utilize peer input to make summative decisions.
2. Don't utilize peers to furnish inside information.
3. Don't select peer observers arbitrarily.

Collegiality

One of the major problems that faces teachers is the loneliness of teaching. The fact that teachers have very little significant contact with other adults during the work day or during the work week creates a problem of morale and a problem for growth. As was illustrated in Figure 3-1, 120 formative observations will do wonders for a school with 20 teachers. Of course, as the number of teachers increases or decreases, the number of formative evaluations will need to be adjusted. Likely results when this recommended number of formative evaluations are made are the following:

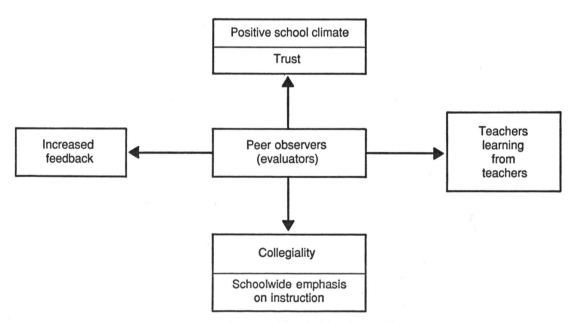

Figure 3-2 Positive Results of Using Peer Observers.

1. Teachers talk more about teaching competencies in the teacher lounge.
2. Teachers observe "good" things in colleagues' classrooms.
3. Teachers have the opportunity to talk with each other about instruction.
4. Teachers and administrators have increased opportunities to work together to improve instruction.

In Figure 3-2, some of the positive results of using peer observers are illustrated.

Trust and collegiality are the characteristics found among the teaching staff in an excellent school. If these organizational prerequisites are in place, the evaluation system and subsequent staff development program—all will be discussed in Chapter 5—will do more to affect the quality of the school positively than, perhaps, any other effort.

Trust of Administrators

It was stated earlier that peer observers will increase trust among staff members, but can peers really be trusted? Can they be trusted with confidentiality? Can they be trusted not to establish a "Good Ol' Colleague" network?

In answer to these questions, experience has proven that peers will act professionally if given professional responsibility. Research leads to the belief however, that there is a tendency for peer evaluators to show a slight upward bias. Peers will give colleagues the benefit of doubt on close calls, but they will not tend to set up coalitions to give each other good evaluations which are not merited.

The goal is for those working under the formative structure to succeed. When threat of criticism is removed, so is the inclination to cheat. When peer observers use a formative instrument, there should be numerous opportunities available for the evaluatee to demonstrate any of the performance indicators. Some classroom procedures do not complement observing certain teaching practices. An obvious example is a class period devoted mostly to testing. When such procedures take place, another observation session should be scheduled.

Teacher Confidence in Peer Observers

Even though trust for the peer evaluators is not a major concern, an initial problem may be acceptance of the peer evaluators by members of the teaching staff. Some possible initial concerns could be:

1. How can a peer observer do anything for me?
2. My students act differently when someone else is in the classroom.
3. Those performance indicators are not germane to my style of teaching or my subject matter.
4. The class is disrupted by so many observations.
5. I need content help, not professional practices.

Most of these concerns are eliminated as teachers become convinced that the formative model is indeed formative. The tendency of students to act differently when someone else is in the room will diminish when frequent observation becomes standard operating procedure. A similar thing will happen with teachers, and frequent observers will not be perceived as a disruptive influence. The call for content help, as opposed to generic teaching practices, is often a diversion tactic used by very structured, inflexible teachers. Every school has those who teach subject matter rather than students. Often, these teachers are part of the informal power structure, and the effort required to bring them "along" is worthwhile. Finally, it may be advisable to allow teachers to opt out of the peer model participation. There will probably be a few teachers who will wish not to participate. For them, all formative requirements should remain, but members of the administrative team could do the observations.

Skepticism can be reduced among these resistant teachers if the treaining offered relates to the generic teaching practices used. Of course, if teachers are involved in identifying the generic practices, then much resistance is eliminated.

PEER SELECTION AND TURNOVER

The selection of peers is an important part of the peer evaluation procedure. Peer selection must be perceived as fair. Of equal importance is that the position of peer observer be as inclusive as possible.

Selection

Possibly the most critical aspect of peer selection is to avoid alienating the teaching staff by making decisions which appear arbitrary or based on favoritism. Selection must be made by the teachers themselves, or an objective criteria must be devised.

A first step might be to determine who is interested in becoming a peer observer. To be a peer observer requires extra time and commitment, and for this reason, some members of the staff may decline the offer. To help secure an adequate number of peer observers, you may wish to offer a realistic salary stipend. This extra pay for extra motivation helps toward solving the linear nature of teaching, whereby promotion requires leaving the profession, which is so detrimental to the morale of highly motivated professionals.

Once the volunteers are identified, you may find it necessary to reduce their number because of the limited number of positions allocated. The elimination process may be accomplished by establishing a point system using certain criteria. Some criteria for which points may be assigned are shown in Figure 3-3.

The goal is to establish a point system which will differentiate among teachers—all of whom may have the potential of becoming excellent observers. Even a selection instrument may cause morale problems if the teachers perceive the criteria as unfair. To avoid this, a committee composed of teachers who are not interested in becoming observers could be helpful. The responsibilities of this committee would be developing selection criteria and assigning to each an allocation of points.

Some of the criteria suggested in the figure need explanation—for example, past year's grade distribution. A prerequisite quality to search for in an observer may be the quality of ensuring that all students succeed. (This quality of wanting others to succeed would be helpful for a formative procedure.) This quality could be assessed on the basis of past performance—the previous year's grade distribution. For example, if 90 percent of student grades were "C" or better, add points for the prospective peer observer. If more than 15 percent of the students received grades below "C," deduct points. (The appropriate percentages can be set locally.) A similar procedure can be designed for the past two-years' attendance.

Turnover

Making the position of peer observer as inclusive of as many teachers as possible will mitigate the disappointment of those not selected initially. This procedure is accomplished through a turnover policy.

The turnover policy is based on selecting peer observers to serve just two or three consecutive years. This policy creates vacancies and opportunities. In schools, and particularly in secondary schools, there is a tendency for those who achieve status positions to assume ownership of such positions. This should not be allowed to happen with the position of peer observer for three reasons:

1. The program should be moving and dynamic.
2. The training component is, perhaps, one of the most significant aspects of the peer observer program. To have training for as many teachers as possible is very desirable.
3. If there are eventual opportunities for all who wish to become peer observers to do so, the program gains acceptance.

CONSIDERATIONS FOR SELECTING PEER OBSERVERS

CRITERIA

POINTS
(to be assigned locally)

1. Experience

    3–5 years   _____

    5–10 years   _____

2. Advanced degree   _____

3. Course work in past year   _____

4. Past year's grade distribution   _____

5. Past two-years' attendance   _____

6. Extra responsibilities assumed
   in past years   _____

Figure 3-3

These goals can be accomplished by establishing a turnover policy which requires each peer observer to relinquish the position for at least one year after two or three consecutive years of service. This policy will help give teachers who were not selected or who did not wish to serve initially a chance to serve at a later date.

With a rotation policy, more teachers will be exposed to observer training. As more teachers receive training in the competencies of effective teaching and have a chance to observe other teachers, both observers and those being observed will grow from the experience. In most schools, almost half the staff will have obtained observer training within just a few years. A common language will be developed among staff members, and a school-wide acceptance of the program will be the end result.

SHOULD PEERS HAVE RELEASED TIME?

How can peer observers find time to observe? This question, usually posed at the early stages of plan development, often causes concerns which prevent further consideration of the use of peer observers. The usual assumption is that, with limited planning time available during the school day, teachers will not have time to observe others. Even though this is a valid concern, it should not be allowed to override the positive reasons for using peer observers.

Much of the in-school planning time of peer observers will be required for making observations. This means that additional out-of-school work will be required. This extra work is the reason that peer observers should be paid a salary stipend. Released time from teaching responsibilities is another way to give peer observers time to observe.

Allowing excessive released time for teacher observers creates school problems, since teachers cannot teach unless they are in the classroom. Too much absence from class detracts from the learning opportunities of the students. For this reason any proposed plan based on releasing observers from class to accomplish *all* the observations should be discouraged. Some released time, perhaps two days per year, can be viewed as a reasonable compromise for making observations.

Assume that an observer must make 18 observations per year, which would require about 70 hours of work. The observer must allocate time for a preconference, the observation, a time for the "write-up," and for a postconference. The observer can do a portion of this work after school hours, but must make the 18 observations during class time. A projected work schedule for a peer observer might resemble the schedule shown in Figure 3-4.

A peer observer can conduct three or four actual observations on a released day and use the remainder of the day to write his or her observations. Separate time for writing of the observations is required, because most observers cannot observe and write coherently at the same time. The writing time is required to convert hastily written notes into a readable document. Figure 3-5 is an example of an actual observation. (Note that the essential techniques of instruction actually have 12 performance indicators.)

Month One	Month Two	Month Three	Month Four	Month Five	Month Six
Training and tandem observations					
	Four complete observations				
		Six complete observations 1 released day			
			Eight compl. observations 1 released day		
				"Catch-up" month	
					Any reobservations requested

Figure 3-4 Sample Work Schedule for Peer Observer.

TEACHER'S NAME: <u>K. Carlisle</u>   DATE: <u>10/15/xx</u>

OBSERVER: <u>B. Adamson</u>

Professional Practice 2— Essential Techniques of Instruction

1. *Teaching materials are organized prior to the time of instruction.*
   Overhead projector, transparency, marker, beans, and paper numbers ready for lesson. Extension cord was ready and out of student walkway.

2. *Expectations of behavior, routines, and learning are explained.*
   "We're going to work on numbers." "We have something new and different today . . ." "I want Miss Wright's class to tiptoe out."

3. *The room arrangement is monitored to ensure students can hear and see the teacher during instruction.*
   Yarn was taped to floor to show students where to sit. Children sat on this yarn facing the blackboard for this lesson. Teacher sat directly behind students.

4. *Transitions between activities minimize loss of instructional time.*
   The group was "lining up" by rows between class change. "I'm going to start with the third row." "Okay?" "Last row, follow them." New group waited in designated place until teacher motioned them in. An activity was on desk so students could start.

5. *Nonverbal communication techniques are used to encourage appropriate behavior.*
   The teacher waited until students were quiet before beginning lesson. *Touched* good student on shoulder and directed him to a seat. *Motioned* to one student to move to a new place on the floor.

6. *The teacher speaks clearly and makes eye contact with students.*
   (Teacher directed students to look up at the board and not at her during lesson.) Many students turned to teacher when responding to questions. Teacher leaned forward to see students.

7. *Teacher circulates among students, accepts student contributions, and stimulates class participation.*

8. *Procedures for instruction and testing are distinguished.*
   No formal testing done. "We're learning about this, so in the first grade you will know about addition."

9. *Opportunities are planned for students to demonstrate initial learning without being graded.*
   Students were involved in orally answering story questions. Math-Their-Way activities included counting beans, etc., and number fact activities provided practice of initial learning.

Figure 3-5

Providing released time is expensive and may not be affordable for all schools or school systems. There are other ways to help peer observers to gain the time necessary for observations. Some possibilities are:

1. Use teacher aides to substitute for a class period at a time when special activities which the aide can accomplish are planned. (This requires avaliability of aid and, of course, support of local policy.)
2. Use teachers with planning periods to help occasionally.
3. Use members of the administrative team as substitutes occasionally—this gives administrators extra credibility.
4. Use parent volunteers.
5. Use auxiliary personnel, such as the school librarian and guidance counselor, if possible.
6. Try to schedule the peer observers' planning period in the morning in elementary schools.

At the secondary-school level, finding time or obtaining coverage for the observers is not as difficult as at the elementary level. In some schools, teachers are permitted to teach only five periods per day because of accreditation requirements. This procedure would allow observers two periods for observation in those schools that schedule a seven-period school day. At the secondary level, it is easier to plan a single-day activity for a volunteer or for another teacher.

If the peer observer program is perceived as an important part of the school program, financial attention is justified. Whether at the elementary or secondary level, a small stipend for teachers who help to release peers for observation is a worthwhile use of funds. The total cost of a peer observer plan could be as little as $200.00 per teacher. This would include stipends for those who help to provide for released time and salary supplements for peer observers. Many schools and school systems presently spend more than this amount on spasmodic and basically ineffective in-service programs.

PEERS AND SCHOOL REFORM

The topic of school reform is always a current issue. School reform has been called by many names: among others, back-to-basics, expanding the curriculum, new science and math, individualized instruction, the child-centered movement, and the excellence movement. There is one predictable variable in these movements: that is, reform is cyclical. A great American trait is to go to extremes in one direction to the neglect of others. This leads to a constant need to divert attention to a neglected area and, thus, to a new reform movement.

Reform movements are usually kindled by changing socioeconomic reality and political expediency. Most reform movements fail to meet the expectancies of those who advocate change. Much of the time, a reform movement can be characterized by, "change in all directions, and then back to business as usual." There are reasons for this failure. An important reason is that reform becomes enveloped by popular political postures. As a result, analyses of changes by research are difficult to make. Another very significant problem is that decisions about teachers and teaching are made without realistic involvement of the teachers. Therefore, the possibility of lasting change is minimized.

Putting a formative evaluation program in the hands of teachers will not solve all of the problems of achieving meaningful change, but it will be an excellent first step. If teachers are to assume a realistic role in evaluation, some changes in thinking must occur. Teachers must be accepted as partners in any enterprise directed toward changing the teaching and, thus, the schools. Teachers must be recognized as basically competent, since most strive to do whatever is necessary to improve learning opportunities for their students. The challenge is to devise systems which create opportunities for teacher involvement in change efforts. It appears that the productive thing is to "do it with teachers, not to teachers."

PEER OBSERVERS AND TEACHER UNIONS

Unions are often accused of trying to preserve the status quo and to protect teachers at the expense of students. It is often said that neither appropriate evaluation nor school reform can be initiated because of teacher unions. To concede that unions and school evaluators must remain in conflict is antiquated thinking. This thinking pervades the mind of the general public and some school boards. Many believe that there are large numbers of incompetent teachers and that evaluation can help weed them out. This philosophy leads to advocacy for a summative evaluation model. Of course, most teachers are reasonably competent and will not benefit from a summative procedure. If this fact is recognized, and the operational philosophy changes, so will some of the potential problems with teacher unions. Teacher self-preservation will probably not cease to be the top priority of unions, but an up-to-date teacher evaluation program can be initiated which will not threaten this need.

Unions can provide certain services for members, but they have failed to meet the goal of making teaching a prestigious profession. Teachers once embraced the union as a means to achieve professional salaries and status. Even after becoming the most highly unionized professionals (80 percent membership), teachers did not attain these goals. Again, this is not to contend that unions can not provide some services for members, but unions, of themselves, cannot achieve professional status for teachers. Teaching must be viewed in a different way for this to happen. For society, this becomes a value or even a moral problem—not a problem which can be solved by collective bargaining and negotiation. Some concepts that can be influenced by peer observers, which will not be resisted by unions, are the following ones:

1. Environments that will increase collegiality and affiliation must be established.
2. The small number of incompetent teachers must be dealt with differently from the large number of teachers in general.
3. Teachers must be involved in the decision-making processes required to improve instruction.
4. The insistence that teachers have status and self-esteem must start at the local level with school boards and administrators.

A system of evaluation, whereby teachers have the role of observers and trainers, can help meet many of these needs. Unions in many localities now appear willing to experiment with new and innovative methods of both formative and summative evaluation.

PEER OBSERVERS AND THE NEW TEACHER

It must be recognized that new teachers tend to be only partially prepared to meet the responsibilities of teaching, although most new teachers are well prepared academically. This is contrary to popular belief. If there is concern for academic ability, the solutions are relatively easy. In reality, few teachers fail in the classroom because of lack of a reasonable grasp of subject matter. Academic failure could be almost totally eliminated if teacher recruiters insisted on carefully reviewing academic credentials, and if pre-employment tests such as the National Teachers Examination were administered.

The Problem with New Teachers

A strong academic background does not confer a guarantee of the ability to teach. Who among the college-educated population has not witnessed an absolutely brilliant professor completely lose an entire class? The problem is not one of knowledge, but the ability to convey knowledge to other human beings.

This inability is the chief probelm with new teachers. In many instances, they have heard about research-based teaching practices, and they have read about research-based teaching practices. However, these new teachers have not seen the practices modeled, and they have not been required to demonstrate the ability to apply these practices.

There is one other problem for the new teacher, which is often overlooked. It is the sheer difficulty of teaching. Most beginning teachers anticipate having a nice, secure job, with meager extrinsic rewards and abundant intrinsic rewards. However, few fail to realize the sheer mental trauma they will face in spending a full day with a class of students. For some teachers, the mental fatigue associated with teaching becomes the most significant problem of adjusting to the new position.

Peer-Training for New Teachers

In the case of new teachers, the peer observers have a special challenge. They must observe for appropriate teaching practices, and they must be observed demonstrating the teaching practices in their own classroom. A dedicated school or school system will conduct a training program for new teachers. The trained peer observers are excellent resources for this program. The preconferences, observations, and postconferences serve as vehicles for beginning teachers to discuss the numerous issues they face. Peer observers can also help beginning teachers by having them observe experienced teachers who can actually model research-based teaching practices.

Perhaps, the most significant factor involved in the process of peers training new teachers is psychological. From the start, there will be an affinity between experienced and beginning teachers. Experienced teachers can help new teachers adjust to the dysfunction of finding that a chosen profession can be much more difficult than anticipated.

The secret of success then is to give beginning teachers a structured system that is based upon practices which work. The structure should be one that systematically models and explains successful methodology, and one that facilitates growth and socialization into the new school culture.

SUMMARY

The use of peer observers can make the evaluation program a school improvement vehicle. Peer observers should be used only to observe other teachers as part of a formative procedure. The observers learn, and those who are observed learn. This environment is one which loses much of the threat traditionally associated with evaluation. Figure 3-5 illustrates some of the components of a system of evaluation where peer observers are used.

The question of trust was discussed from two perspectives: that of the advisability of using teachers for the peer observers; and the other, the relying on peers to evaluate accurately. It is true that initial problems are likely to occur. Some teachers may be skeptical of the value of generic teaching practices and of the prospect of being observed by other teachers, many of whom may be teaching in different subject areas or grade levels. Any problem with teacher acceptance is likely to disappear when teachers see that:

1. They are involved in identifying teaching competencies.
2. The peer evaluation system is formative and, as such, nonthreatening.

3. Most problems encountered by teachers involve the generic teaching practices.

4. The atmosphere of the school changes and "what works" in teaching becomes the focal point of this new school environment.

Peer observers will gain the respect of the administrators, the school board, and the public in general, as positive changes become evident. Peer observers tend to show a slight positive bias in observing other teachers, but since formative evaluation is not designed to "get the incompetent," the problem is not significant. Having teachers observed by their peers is a very desirable way to enhance their growth.

In choosing peer observers, the perception of fairness is critical. Also, there are two reasons for making the position of peer observer inclusive:

1. Morale is boosted if all teachers understand that they have the opportunity to become peer observers.

2. Orderly rotation of the peer observers ensures that many teachers receive observer training. This procedure facilitates the development of a common school-wide language and enhances professional fraternity among teachers.

The cost for a peer evaluation program is often less than that of some in-service activities frequently used. Salary supplements are important for peer observers, since serving in this capacity takes extra time. Becoming a peer observer is an ideal way to address the linear nature of teaching by providing an outlet for those who are motivated to seek achievement and recognition.

Finally, the role of a peer observer in the initiation of the new teachers was examined. It was suggested that peer observers might serve as models for the new teachers. Peer observers are also apt to be readily accepted by new teachers, who will be working towards demonstrating competent teaching practices required of them.

An evaluation system utilizing peer observers can help correct a serious flaw in the training of most new teachers. This flaw can be characterized as the "read about / hear about" method of teaching generic teaching practices. New teachers receive their academic instruction from those who understand teaching from an analytical perspective. Often, it does not occur to these purveyors of knowledge that new teachers are more likely to emulate the teaching behaviors they observe rather than those that they read about. When those charged with training prospective teachers use the "chalk and talk" method, new teachers are likely to learn and emulate the behavior. This lack of proper modeling means that new teachers must be retaught during their first year of teaching. Peer observers can provide outstanding help in this endeavor.

chapter 4

TRAINING EVALUATORS

The training evaluators is one of the most significant activities that can improve teacher evaluation. The implications of training evaluators are much broader than merely the imparting of subject matter of skills. The training program for evaluators can be expanded until almost every professional activity is focused toward the goal of effective teaching.

Training is of little value unless a change in behavior occurs. How to make training "stick" is an important concern for all who would exert effort and resources to train evaluators. Some practices in evaluator training which have proven effective will be discussed in this chapter.

Finally, if evaluators understand the basis for helping other professionals to become effective, self-confident, motivated individuals, the purpose of evaluation will be accomplished. Appropriate training methods will help evaluators observe from example how meaningful assistance can be provided.

THE TRAINING FOCUS

The point has been made previously that involvement in the training component of an evaluation system is probably as valuable as the evaluation process itself. Through the training experience, evaluators can learn the latest information about effective teaching. The teaching practices that are in the evaluation program can be modeled, and a common language can be developed. These factors have an impact upon the informal group structure that exists within the school.

Once the evaluation system has been developed, the success of the process depends upon training factors. These are cited in the following checklist:

_____ 1. Ownership created in the development process

_____ 2. Administrative commitment as evidenced by *all* administrators having received initial training

_____ 3. Administrators proficient in all aspects of the evaluation system, as well as in their ability to conduct most of the peer training

_____ 4. A continuing program for all evaluators (peer evaluators and administrators) which incorporates demonstration of modeling and tandem observations

_____ 5. Periodic reinforcement and feedback

Ownership

Ownership begins with a plan to either update or revise the evaluation instrument. Even prior to the plan for updating, a preliminary step might begin with a survey of teachers. The survey is designed to get information about the present system and suggestions for the new system. Figure 4-1 lists some of the questions which might form the basis of a survey instrument. Of course, locally developed questions could be added.

The sample survey questions are designed to reinforce the need to improve the evaluation system. Unless an outstanding system of formative evaluation is in place, most responses will indicate a need to improve an existing system. A first step toward eventual ownership occurs if the initial plan to update the evaluation system follows a survey or a needs assessment of those who are evaluated.

After initial input has indicated a need to improve evaluation, a follow-up survey may be conducted about suggestions for improvement. The follow-up survey can be a questionnaire or a topical discussion for each faculty. As discussed in Chapter 3, local research units will be needed, but the initial suggestions will provide valuable input.

The main avenue to ownership is participation. The training program for administrators and peer observers must impart a sense of ownership. Only when an evaluation instrument becomes "ours" and not "theirs" can the full potential for evaluation be realized.

Administrative Commitment

Modeling and personal example are the best teaching tools. It is unfortunate when expectancies are given and not modeled by administrators. If persons who

Evaluation Survey

YES/NO

_____ 1. The evaluation procedure adequately reflects teaching ability.

_____ 2. The evaluation procedure helps to improve teaching.

_____ 3. Feelings about my professional contribution are enhanced as a result of evaluation.

_____ 4. The evaluation system reinforces the latest research about effective teaching.

_____ 5. Evaluation procedures ultimately result in improved learning opportunities for students.

_____ 6. Adequate opportunity for input into the content of the evaluation procedure is provided.

_____ 7. The person charged with the responsibility of evaluating is qualified for this task.

_____ 8. An evaluation procedure that utilizes the expertise of teachers should be designed.

_____ 9. The staff development program relates to evaluation.

_____ 10. Evaluation serves as a vehicle for improved morale.

Figure 4-1

administer expect others to learn and grow, they need to be visibly engaged in similar activities.

All administrators should be the first who are trained in the use of an evaluation instrument. Often, outside consultants are employed to train administrators. This may not be the best approach if the training involves a locally developed evaluation procedure. The key person who worked in the development of the procedure may be outstanding resource personnel for training. Training teams which include administrators and teachers can be organized. Some advantages of using training teams are as follows:

1. The procedure demonstrates faith in the peer concept.
2. A procedure which ensures involvement and, thus, ownership is developed at the initial stage.
3. Those who helped construct the procedure should be able to model the concepts.

Proficient Administrators

Administrative training should be conducted with the view that local administrators will chair training units which will train peer observers. Proficiency cannot be gained simply by attending a few sessions at which the new evaluation system is explained. Administrators should be able to conduct demonstration lessons, where the competencies sought in the evaluation process are demonstrated. In these training sessions, other administrators should use the new instrument to evaluate their peers.

After all administrators are proficient with the system, a common language is developed, and common expectations are established. Then, training of the peer observers may be undertaken.

A Continuing Program

A practical rule to remember when working with human organizations is that *probelms are never fixed and relationships are never set.* Interpreted, this means that new ways of reacting soon become indistinguisable from old ways, if they are not strengthened by a program of planned reinforcement. The rule means that human relationships must be valued and attended to, if they are to be maintained.

Once the evaluation program is established, training and retraining must be a planned process. Demonstrations and discussions must become part of most administrative meetings. Occasionally, outside consultants could be of benefit once everyone has a grasp of the evaluation system. For example, classroom control may be one of the targeted competencies. A consultant, given the performance indicators of classroom control, can build a presentation around them. There is a reluctance to endorse outside consultants for anything, but consultants can strengthen a plan if expectancies are outlined and accountability carefully upheld.

Reinforcement and Feedback

Too often, a "good" program is initiated and then left in place as if all its goals were accomplished forever. This is the reason for failure of many innovations; such neglect diminishes the effect of a new program of evaluation. Constant reinforcement and feedback are necessary, if competent evaluation is to become the standard way of operating.

Those engaged in evaluation may receive feedback and reinforcement through a management structure specifically designed for this purpose. For example, after initial training is accomplished, each evaluator should conduct several tandem observations per year with another observer—either a peer observer or an administrator. This tandem observation will serve as one of the checks for inter-rater reliability.

> NOTE: The term "inter-rater reliability" is often used as one of the terms for checking the validity and reliability of an evaluation instrument. Checking validity and reliability for an evaluation system that is devoted mainly to formative purposes, and in which specific performance indicators are documented anecdotally, is not as significant as it is with summative evaluation. Outside consultants could be used to conduct research on an evaluation instrument. The reservations previously expressed do not apply here, because there is a considerable difference between research and training.

Tandem observations that are followed by a conference result in reinforcement. Tandem observations also heighten the motivation for perceptions, as each observer naturally seeks to appear competent for the task.

Another kind of follow-up is to have a third party review all observation reports. Principals can review observation reports of peer observers, and central office personnel can review observations for an entire school. The purpose of the review is to be certain that all observers are looking for the same things and to give observers feedback on the observation reports. This review system keeps the evaluation program in high priority. Figure 4-2 shows how such a system might be organized.

A METHOD OF TRAINING

Perhaps the only way to ensure competent evaluations is to model appropriate procedures and to have observers demonstrate the observation instrument and receive appropriate feedback (coaching). Those being trained should be able to

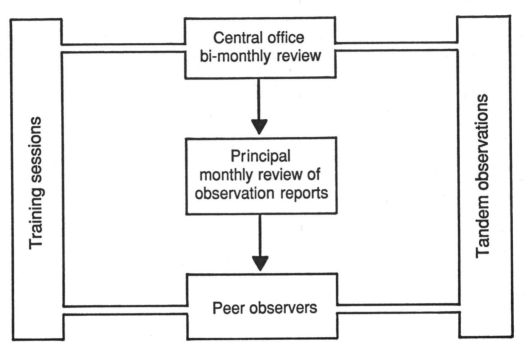

Figure 4-2 Evaluation Review System.

model the teaching competencies and use the observation instrument. The training is accomplished through team work, as is shown in Figure 4-3.

At first glance, Figure 4-3 appears to be quite complicated. The procedure outlined is viewed as essential for appropriate training of observers and becomes easy to administer with experience.

The most qualified trainers available are those who constructed the evaluation instrument and identified the teacher competencies. The training teams created use these individuals to conduct observer training. The primary training teams are composed mostly of those who developed the evaluation instrument.

The statements in Boxes (C) and (D) of Figure 4-3 cite the components which distinguish this training process from the usual in-service. Modeling and using the evaluation are the two components. For example, if one of the competencies is "constructing appropriate lesson plans," the training team designs a lesson plan which contains the components expected. The team teaches from this plan and attempts to model the actual use of all components (C). Then, part of the training team evaluates the instructor by using the evaluation instrument (D).

Even the preconference and the postconference are modeled. The members of the team who conduct the observations also conduct the postconference and preconference. In this manner, conferencing skills are also modeled.

Beginning with the secondary training teams, those who have been through the initial training conduct training for the remaining competencies in the system. Preconferences and postconferences are also modeled. The initial training team remains with the group to offer coaching and to serve as members of the secondary

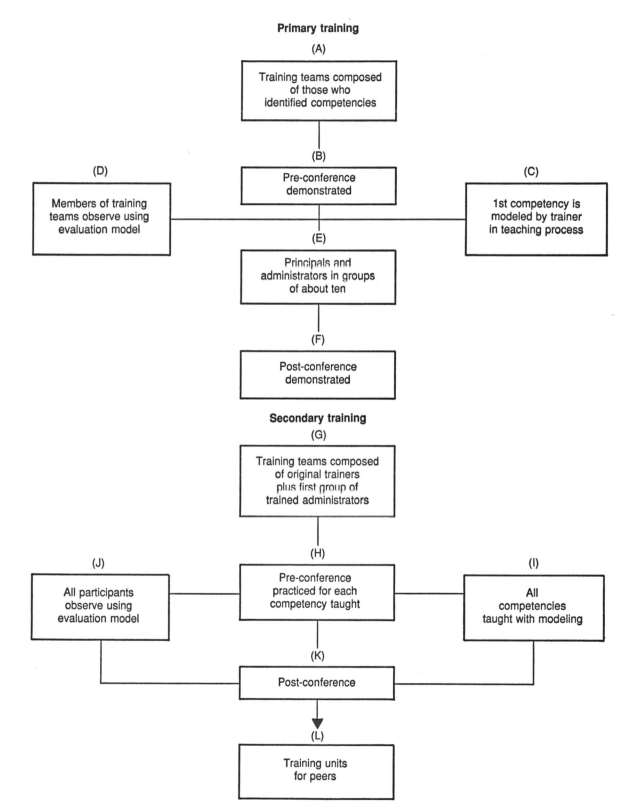

Figure 4-3 Training Observers.

training teams (G). Ultimately, training is conducted for all teacher competencies. Preconferences and postconferences are held each time a competency is presented, and presenters are expected to model the competency and the accompanying performance indicators while teaching them to the group. Someone in the group always evaluates the instruction, and this evaluation is discussed in the postconference.

Through this method of training, all administrators will teach the same material in the same manner when the teams are formed to train peer observers (L). After the initial training, periodic reinforcement and retraining must be scheduled. Note that even an outstanding program will revert to mediocrity without constant attention. As mentioned earlier, nothing stays "fixed" in the realm of human organizations. In fact, the ecology of human organizations is very similar to the nautral succession found in plant ecology--that is, both will revert to a natural state if left uninterrupted.

Preconference—A Controversy

There is some disagreement about whether or not a preconference should be included as a part of every observation. If both the observer and teacher are comfortable with the evaluation procedure, and if both understand precisely what will be demonstrated and what will be observed, a preconference might be omitted. However, this is usually not the case; therefore, the preconference is recommended.

Exporting the Training Model

Once all administrators and supervisors are trained, the procedure can be exported to the peer observers. The training units are now composed of members of the original training teams and administrative staff. It is important to utilize the teachers who served on the research units that devised the evaluation system and those who served on the original training team or teams. With both teachers and administrators involved in training peers, the following advantages are realized:

1. Recognizing the expertise of teachers to conduct staff development boosts morale.
2. The trainers have ownership and pride in the system, and these feelings are sensed by the trainees.
3. When an administrator and teacher work together as trainers, each recognizes the competence of the other.

Figure 4-4 summarizes how research units initially train and then combine unit members with members of administrative and supervisory staff for the remainder of the training.

CHANGING TRADITIONAL REALITY

Some of the concepts advocated in the preceding section differ from those associated with traditional evaluation systems and the training needed to support effective implementation. A few of the traditional practices that we discourage are the following:

1. A "mixed" summative and formative evaluation instrument or procedure that is supposed to help weed out incompetencies and to help the teacher grow professionally
2. An evaluation instrument which lists desired characteristics, but does

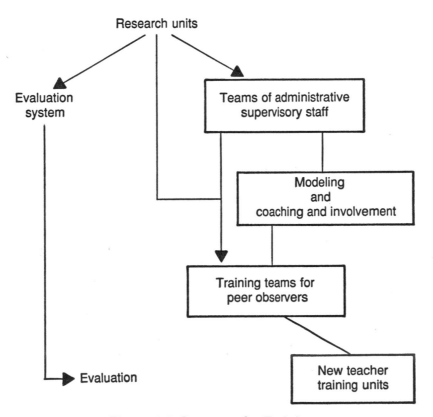

Figure 4-4 Structure for Training.

not define, with any precision, how degree of accomplishment is to be measured

3. An evaluation instrument devised without input from teachers and principals, or one handed down from year to year that incorporates little or no new research about effective teaching practices

4. Assumptions that the administrative and supervisory staff are competent to evaluate without a continuing program of training

5. Formative and summative evaluation plans that are the responsibility of the same evaluator

6. An evaluation system based on only one or two class observations per year

7. A formative evaluation protocol, for which problems are identified and solutions prescribed

8. A ranking of teachers by category, such as unsatisfactory, improvement needed, average, above average, or excellent

These evaluation practices generally serve one purpose well—they help the evaluator believe that the necessary job of evaluation has been accomplished. It should be noted that new research about effective teaching has been available for a number of years, yet most teachers continue to use traditional methodology and insulate themselves from these new ideas. This is not to demean traditional practice. There is new information, however, which is supported by top quality research, that should be incorporated into practice.

Perhaps traditional evaluation supports traditional teaching practice. Evaluation is largely perceived as assessment of what *has* happened—standing alone and with no relationship to staff development, staff morale, or staff effectiveness in working with students.

If traditional reality is to be changed, evaluation is the place to begin. The formative model advocated is a model that encourages the acceptance of teachers as true professionals, a model that can be used to identify research-based teaching practices, and one that facilitates the adoption of effective practices into teaching. The possible contribution of peers has been previously discussed, and a training method for peers and administrative and supervisory personnel has been outlined. If peers are to be utilized in evaluation, some restructuring of roles will be required. This restructuring and its implications will be discussed next.

Central Office Supervisory Personnel

With the adoption of the formative model, the role of central office supervisory personnel will become more that of curriculum specialists and trainers. It is fairly common for central office supervisors to assist in the evaluative process.

Through the use of peer evaluators, the evaluation responsibilities of supervisors can be reduced. Peer observers can be given the additional responsibility to observe and use the formative instrument.

Heavy emphasis is placed on generic teaching practices. Most problems arising from incompetent teaching can be derived from the inability of teachers to perform one or more of the generic practices which are essential for competent performance. This aspect of teaching is sometimes called the pedagogy of teaching.

As stated previously, very few teachers lack the necessary basic academic background and ability. There is one catch to this statement, however. Unless teachers understands the scope and sequence of subject content, the planning for student outcomes will be inadequate or incomplete. Too often, this area of teacher performance is left to chance; but with generic aspects of teaching attended to by **peers, the supervisor** can direct his or her attention to subject content.

The new role of subject matter specialist or supervisor will require new approaches to supervision. Supervisory observations will change, for their focus will be entirely supervisory in nature. The Supervisor will become interested in what is being taught, how it relates to the teacher's goals, and if both are appropriate in scope and sequence. If help is needed, the supervisor will give assistance and serve as facilitator—helping to secure resources, materials, and outside assistance. The supervisor will make recommendations for course work, if needed. All of this activity is outside the evaluation process.

The suggestion to remove the supervisor from the evaluation process (with a few exceptions discussed in Chapter 7) and to give the supervisor subject matter responsibility may cause concern among some educators, but this procedure will result in an effective utilization of personnel. Figure 4-5 shows some of the traditional responsibilities of supervisors. It is contrasted with the change in role that might occur with the adoption of a formative evaluation system which utilizes peer observers.

The change in role requires supervisors to take on the responsibility of being true instructional leaders. Supervisors will have to understand specific subject content related to areas of specialty, and they will need to be familiar with all the generic teaching practices identified in the evaluation plan.

Not only will supervisors need to be conversant with the generic teaching practices but also they will need to teach the practices, model them, and coach others in their use. Supervisors and other central office personnel have long lamented that bureaucratic responsibilities prevent them from being the instructional leaders they would like to be. A formative evaluation system with peer observers and a major emphasis on training may help to solve, at least, some of these problems.

The Principal

With the formative and summative evaluations separated, the principal will have three roles: (1) to coordinate the work of peer observers, and to make sure the

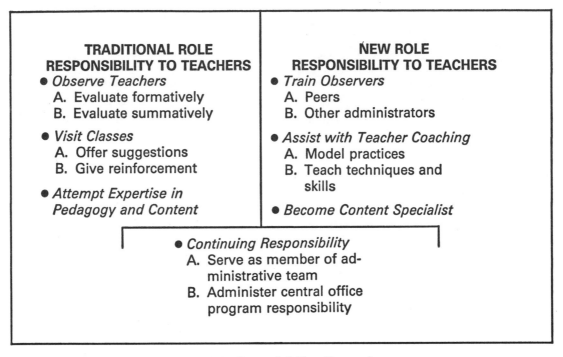

Figure 4-5 Central Office Supervisors.

formative program is working; (2) to administer a summative evaluation system; and (3) to keep emphasis on training.

The principal should be the only evaluator that has some responsibility in both summative and formative evaluations. This is compatible with his or her role as being the person who is ultimately in charge of the school. In the formative role, the principal does not actually evaluate. He is the recipient of the peer evaluation reports. Based on the reports received, the principal and teacher decide which new professional practices should be emphasized. If the teacher does not complete the professional practices attempted, the principal serves as a facilitator for goal setting.

The principal's role in the summative process is to establish a summative schedule for all teachers. (It would be difficult, and probably useless, to evaluate all teachers summatively each year.) The principal solicits help for those who have a problem meeting the summative criteria (contract, pay raise, promotion, certificate, etc.) and secures assistance in the preparation of appropriate documentation for those teachers who eventually demonstrate that they can't or won't perform at the minimum level. (See Chapter 7.)

To coordinate the training program, the principal must make the school a place for professional learning, as well as for student learning. Some suggestions are given which might help the principal in this endeavor:

1. The principal should appoint a professional development committee.
2. The principal must be certain that the evaluation system serves as a guide for the professional development agenda.

3. The principal needs a budget from central sources for professional development—a minimum of $2.00 per student enrolled is suggested.

4. Training activities should be conducted at least twice a month.

The principal will need to work closely with the central office supervisory staff to provide the training needed. Additional suggestions about successful staff development will be given in Chapter 5.

Communication

It is essential to consider communication when contemplating ways of establishing peer observer/teacher relationships. From the beginning, it is helpful to define communication as a "selling procedure used to negotiate a particular purpose." With peer observers, the product to sell is assistance. Peer observers must be able to provide observation feedback to the teacher in a manner that sells the process and ensures that it is accepted as a procedure for the improvement of instruction.

An objective description based solely on what was observed is not the chief goal of evaluation. There must be a focus on evaluation's purpose. In this context, the purpose is to change reality—i.e., for the teacher to abandon any behaviors that do not work and to adopt effective practices. For example, a teacher's performance might be characterized as average, because the teacher did not demonstrate some key components of effective practice. To communicate reality (i.e., only average performance) may cost the opportunity to change reality.

You may ask, "How can peers communicate inadequate performance?" Also, "How can peers serve as catalysts for the adoption of effective practice?" Each of these questions get to the very crux of why there is reluctance to use peers and to what the main objective of peer training should be.

The model of evaluation most familiar to educators is to "identify what is wrong and develop a strategy or target to remediate the problem." Dispelling the notion that this procedure could possibly be effective must be part of the new reality. If the job of the evaluator is simply to identify problems and set targets, effective communication does not develop, and the function of peer observers becomes a useless one. Perhaps, a discussion of each question will help to develop a workable approach for effective communication in the evaluative process.

How Can Peers Communicate Inadequate Performance?

The job of communicating inadequate performance, when it must be done, belongs to administration and is part of the summative process. If peer evaluators function to identify problems, they will be resented by the other teachers. Peers should be utilized to identify teacher strengths. Take another look at the example of a peer assessment (see Figure 3-5). Notice that the peer observer documented only the positive actions of the teacher which demonstrated each of the performance indicators. Also note that the observer saw nothing which demonstrated Item 7. It is interesting to consider how much information a blank space can convey! The teacher response to this blank space is likely to be one of the following:

1. "You missed this . . . Let me tell you what I did which demonstrated competence in this practice."
2. "You missed this, but I can't remember when or how I demonstrated it."
3. "This was not a good lesson for demonstration. Will you come back?"
4. "How can I demonstrate this practice?"

All of these responses open the door for another visit or for assistance. With the "positive only" structure for peer observers, the problems of communication are lessened, but the agenda for improving instruction remains intact.

How Can Peers Serve as Catalysts for the Adoption of Effective Practice?

Modeling that is followed by guided practice is the most effective way to teach new teaching behaviors. The old practice of "report and exhort" is an exercise in futility, as it results in little or no change. Peer observers can either model the desired behavior or refer the matter to another teacher who can model the desired skill. Peer observers can also give guided practice to help teachers who missed performance indicators or skills in the first observation.

Training in communication skills must be offered to peer observers. Peer observers must be able to communicate from a formative perspective. This ability is, perhaps, the most critical quality for successful peer evaluations. Some guidelines for peer communication follow:

1. Peer observers should not attempt to project authority or competence. Authority is not congruent with the formative model, and competency will be recognized without the "positioning" which gets in the way of relationships.
2. Peer observers should avoid the use of criticism, since it invariably becomes the focus of observation review and diverts attention from problem solving. Criticism is difficult to handle when given by a position leader. It is devastating to a positive relationship when given by a peer.
3. Peer observers must avoid "teacher lounge talk." This means they

should avoid making comments about a teacher who has been observed. The exception is the sharing of a novel idea or technique which was observed.

4. Peer observers must become listeners as well as observers. The comments of the teacher in discussing the lesson, both before and after observation, usually suggest how the peer observers may be of assistance. Training in listening techniques is desirable.

A training program for observational skills will not of itself ensure success for an evaluation program. Peer observers must be adequate communicators. Each observer must learn to place the instructional goal in top priority—the needs of self must be placed in a secondary position.

The need for the peer observer to abandon temporarily most individual needs is a problem of serious concern. Teachers have long sought professional respect, and most teachers can sight many instances where their professional expertise has not been recognized. Frequently, the teacher manifests this need for recognition by playing the part of expert, the part of critic, or by attempting to project an aloofness from the mundane concerns of "typical teachers." These inappropriate "need" fulfilling behaviors on the part of a peer observer can quickly kill an observer's effectiveness.

The peer observers must receive support and recognition from the administration to help reduce any "need deficit" which might give rise to status-gathering behaviors. The importance of becoming a facilitator of need fulfillment in others should receive special emphasis in peer observer training.

SUMMARY

In order for peer evaluators to contribute meaningfully to the evaluation process, a peer-observer training program must be of high priority. It is noteworthy that the terms, peer observer and peer evaluator, are used interchangeably. The reason for this is that some educators may view any observation in the classroom as an evaluation. Those who are familiar with formative assessment will be more at ease with the term peer observer. Technically, and considering the role advocated for peers, the term observer is the most appropriate.

The process of training peer observers will be successful if certain components are in place. These components are:

1. A sense of ownership
2. Commitment of the administration
3. Administrators who demonstrate commitment by becoming experts in the use of the evaluation instrument.

4. Trainers who can model the teaching practices
5. A system of training which involves reinforcement and feedback through a coaching process

Next, a method of training is suggested. Those who write or review the evaluation instrument are to first train all administrators in its interpretation and use. Then, the initial trainers join administrators in forming teams to train the peer observers. This method of training ensures that all administrators are expert in using the new evaluation instrument. Note that at least one-half of the original training team (those who played a primary role in writing the professional practices in the new instrument) will be outstanding classroom teachers.

A new way of viewing evaluative reality is advocated. The sole purpose of formative evaluation is to improve instruction. The traditional "report and exhort" type of evaluation is not productive. New concepts which take into account human motivation and which enhance an outcome-oriented approach to motivation are needed.

The traditional role of central office supervisor needs to change. Peer observers can relieve the supervisory staff of the task observing the generic teaching practices, and the supervisors can become teachers of other practitioners, as well as content-area specialists.

Finally, with training in communication skills, peers can be trained to lead professional growth without communicating negative reactions about the performance of others. Peer observers must model desired performance and coach others in attaining these skills.

chapter 5

THE EVALUATION INSTRUMENT AS A BASIS FOR STAFF DEVELOPMENT

Other than teacher evaluation, staff development is the most "fertile field" for improving the quality of educational practice in the schools. It might be noted that a "fertile field" standing fallow is of little use. In fact, if left uncultivated, it will grow weeds. The "weeds" of staff development are well known. They can be equated to the perceptions among the teaching staff that most staff development efforts are: (1) poorly planned, (2) not relevant, (3) useless, and (4) generate meetings that are boring to attend.

One of the primary problems with staff development is that it is usually treated as an independent entity. Schools and school systems usually have evaluation programs, instructional programs, financial plans, and staff development programs, but each is treated as if they are separate and nonrelated functions. Why are these functions not incorporated as interdependent parts of a single effort directed toward student outcomes?

It is suggested in this chapter that staff development is derived from evaluation. Of course, evaluation and all components of the curriculum delivery system must be interrelated and directed toward the central focus of the school or school system.

The primary concern is that teacher evaluation be supported by staff development. For this to be properly accomplished, a different way of viewing the functions of a school, as they relate to curriculum delivery, must be adopted. A "curriculum delivery systems" approach to planning is discussed below.

Other practical aspects of staff development are also discussed, such as its purpose and, of course, how to make a staff development plan work. Finally, some political aspects of staff development that merit attention are treated.

CURRICULUM DELIVERY SYSTEMS

As can be observed from Figure 5-1, there are several functions of a school system or school which can and should be meshed into a coordinated unit. Each of these functions is of major importance; and in a typical bureaucratic organization, each is represented by a director or, in some cases, an assistant superintendent. A tremendous waste of effort and finances occurs when each of these functions is administered out of a separate office and when there is only cursory consideration given to the other functions. With a lack of coordination for the curriculum delivery system, the Critical focus required for attending to curriculum delivery systems becomes diffuse.

Focusing of the curriculum delivery system should start with a staff development program based upon the evaluation system. Then, of course, teacher evaluation should reflect the goals of the instructional program. Financial planning must support the entire effort. Finally, the personnel component must be included, because the total focus should be supported by the employment and positioning of teaching personnel whose philosophies and abilities are compatible with performance expectancies.

Since staff development is the primary topic of this chapter, more attention will be paid to this component and how it supports evaluation than the other parts of

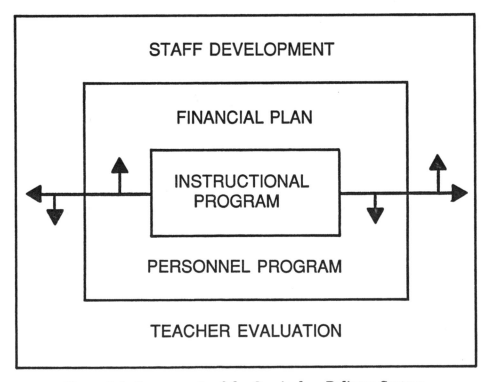

Figure 5-1 Components of the Curriculum Delivery System.

the curriculum delivery system. However, the entire scope of the curriculum delivery system is treated briefly, so that the reader may consider the kind of total approach which is needed and the major components which must be coordinated.

Staff development should rarely be conducted separtely from the other purposes related to the school or school-system focus. This is not the case with current practice. However, it is encouraging when several important aspects of successful staff development are widely observed. These include the following:

1. Choices given to teachers in selecting activities.
2. In-service for specific performance objectives.
3. Involvement of teachers in planning.
4. Released time or pay for extra time to teachers for their involvement in staff development.

There is little evidence to indicate that many staff development programs in use fully support teacher evaluation or that there are widespread initiatives to coordinate the entire curriculum delivery system.

If the evaluation system is derived from local research units, as was previously suggested, then teacher evaluation will be based upon identifying the existence of competencies which are characteristic of effective teaching. It is obvious that the staff development program should be built around these competencies. Programs and initiatives in staff development should be planned only when a careful analysis is made of the needs of teaching personnel, as these needs relate to competencies sought in evaluation.

For illustration purposes, assume that the instructional focus of a school system is to implement a performance-based system of instruction and that such system is to be supported by the mastery learning philosophy and Madeline Hunter's mastery teaching strategies. The system's evaluation program should center on competencies which support the implementation of mastery learning, Hunter techniques, and teaching-to-performance goals.

The staff development program should be centered around the identified competencies. The financial planning would involve arranging funds for each school to initiate staff development and funds for centrally sponsored activities. During the years of implementation, the personnel department would recruit administrators and teachers who could complement the instructional focus.

In considering the mission of a school or school system in terms of a coordinated curriculum delivery system, several questions must be resolved by the local staff. These are the following:

1. What is the central focus (primary goal)?
2. Does the evaluation system reflect the focus?
3. Does staff development support evaluation?

4. What financial resources are needed to support a central focus?

5. What contribution is needed for the employment of personnel?

6. How can financial planning support individual school initiatives and division-wide activities?

Coordination of activities appears to be a straightforward task, but it isn't. Look at finances as an example. Directing financial resources appears to be an easy part of coordination. The initial impression is, "Surely resources could be raised for coordination." However, to involve finances in this effort means to adopt a new way of doing business. A look at typical practice illustrates how much change is required.

A nationwide sampling of the evaluation programs used by school systems was collected as part of the preparation for writing this book. The school systems sampled were divided into two population groups—those with less than 20,000 students, and those with more. A review of approximately thirty evaluation systems led to three conclusions:

1. All were basically similar.

2. Little, if any, sign of application of the central focus could be found.

3. There was little indication that evaluation was related to staff development or anything else.

Typically, those involved with each component of the curriculum delivery system exercise considerable autonomy in the submitting of their respective proposed budgets. Very little attention is paid to the other component agencies. For each, coordination would entail a small loss of autonomy. More importantly, it would mean that each would need to spend more time coordinating activities with persons involved in each component area.

A departure from typical practice is required for all components of the curriculum delivery system to be connected. It is, indeed, challenging to visualize the possibilities for accomplishment if all efforts are directed toward a central focus or mission.

STAFF DEVELOPMENT AND THE BROAD VIEW

The public perceives all evaluation to be for summative purposes. They often perceive staff development as "teacher work days"—additional extra time for teachers who already work short hours and have summers "off." Taking a broad view of staff development is a starting point for correcting misconceptions about evaluation and teacher in-service.

The "broad view" means that staff development should be perceived as more than a teacher activity. It should involve changing behavior, accomplishing goals, and making school a better place for children. If staff development is to have significant impact on the quality of the schools, it must be perceived of as the primary avenue to change. It must involve both professional staff and support staff. Comprehensive involvement is another result of a central focus.

Some of the most important authorities on schooling are often ignored. These are the various staff persons, such as cafeteria workers, custodians, bus drivers, mechanics, and secretaries. In the average school system, support staff is roughly equivalent in number of employees to the professional staff. Support staff personnel are called "authorities" because they usually know a great deal about what happens in their schools. Their neighbors and friends often believe they know the entire school story. In fact, they trust them even more than they trust the school principal does. To involve these persons in staff development is another part of the broad view.

If support personnel are trusted by some to tell the school story, then it is important that they know as much of the story as possible. In-service about the focus of the school or school system is appropriate. It is also important that support personnel have an understanding of how the professional staff is evaluated. It is regrettable that support staff members are often viewed as the uninformed and as those who can derive benefits from staff development only about such matters as how to clean more efficiently or how to keep U.S.D.A. commodity records.

When a major focus is identified, a primary goal should be to take a broad view for staff development. The first question should be, "Who else can we involve in this effort?"

MAKING STAFF DEVELOPMENT WORK

Staff development has three primary purposes:

1. To change teaching practices
2. To change student outcomes
3. To change teacher perception

Of course, if the evaluation system represents the latest research about effective teaching and if the overriding purpose of staff development is to support evaluation, then the sequence of staff development which is directed toward change might resemble Figure 5-2.

The most frequently used word in Figure 5-2 is *change*. It would be the choice term if staff development needed to be described in a single word. Consider also the numbered items in Figure 5-2. Their sequential order underscores the way change occurs for most teachers.

If teachers try a new practice and notice better student outcomes, this success will cause a change in their perceptions about teaching. The change in their

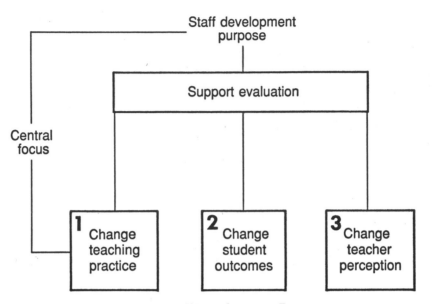

Figure 5-2 Staff Development Purpose.

perceptions can involve the realization that the new practice works, or it can involve viewing students in a more optimistic manner than before.

The mini-model of change illustrated in Figure 5-2 is exactly the reverse of the usual direction of staff development. The order usually followed is 3–1–2 (perception, performance, outcomes). Through the use of this incorrect model, the desired change is seldom achieved. The typical sequence involves the teacher attending "in-service," enjoying the company of fellow teachers during the re-freshment break, and returning to the classroom for "business as usual."

It might be said that the best part of typical "in-service" is the refreshment break. The validity of this assertion exceeds that of "poking fun" at an obsolete practice. In reality, the refreshment break is practically the only time some teachers have to enjoy fraternal relationships. The short conversations of the refreshment break help to break teachers' psychological isolation from other adults with similar interests. These short encounters have been known to lead to intellectual stimula-tion and renewed motivation. They sometimes result in teachers taking the risks involved in changing their teaching behaviors.

Words to Action

As implied, the primary problem of staff development is to make a differ-ence. Many hours of staff development time are spent with some of the most knowledgeable persons in the field of education. These "staff developers" include slick motivational experts, college professors, and directors of successful innova-tions. Of course, the problem is that most teachers are already motivated. They know most of the subject matter presented by the professor, but still they resist innovation. One of the primary problems then is the dissonance between the need system of individual teachers and the need fulfilling ability of those conducting staff development. It is helpful to look at ways this dissonance might be reduced—thereby, converting words to action.

It must be realized that teaching is much more complex than is normally assumed. Teaching is not only complex but also taxing and consuming. It is not uncommon to hear, "He talks like a teacher." This statement arises from the fact that the teacher becomes the person. The making of a "teacher-person" results from an array of complicated factors. A teacher's knowledge base is achieved through experience gained and years of endeavor. This implies that simplistic perceptions of effective practices or a few explanations of these practices do not produce expert teachers.

The question becomes, "How can the resources of time, finances, and effort be directed to activities which might make a differnce?" Even though teaching is complex, and research about what works for the development of an effective teacher is incomplete, the research represents the best avenue available for improving teaching practice. In fact, more information has been learned about teaching in the last decade than in the previous fifty years. Indeed, failure to utilize this information is shortsighted. The direction of staff development should include emphasis on (1) the area of school or school division focus, (2) The research-based practices of effective teaching (which should be reflected in the evaluation system), and (3) specific content areas, such as writing across the curriculum or teaching advanced placement biology.

There are three primary administrative requisites for building effective staff development programs. These are the following:

1. Set the parameters of all staff development.
2. Make certain recipients of staff development are involved in decision making.
3. Provide adequate opportunities for participant selection of activities.

In an evaluation system, the establishing of parameters for staff development that relates to the needs of the school or school system is essential. An obvious question arises when the administration does this: "If administration sets the parameters, how can realistic involvement in decision making occur?"

To make decisions within a policy framework is not unusual—the principal and the superintendent operate in this manner daily. A staff development committee can exercise significant professional input within the established parameters. For example, the committee may recommend a balance between pedagogical and content-oriented effort, establish priority for a competency in the evaluation system, or stress staff development activities that can effectively support the current school focus.

Effective staff development can occur only if the participants want to be involved. Self-selection and freedom of choice help ensure a more positive involvement than might be the case otherwise.

If the requisites discussed above are administered with enlightenment and sensitivity, they will go quite far in eliminating some of the major criticisms of staff development. These criticisms include the following:

1. Lack of relevance
2. Lack of specificity of objectives
3. Lack of planning
4. Lack of interest

Gaining initial acceptant for staff development will help recipients become willing learners. However, this acceptance is only a small part of productive staff development, since having staff members learn different facts does not mean that they will adopt different behaviors.

MAKING CHANGE PERMANENT

With the stage set for staff development and with teachers as willing recipients, teachers should then be given the most current information. Only a very small portion of this information will be used or permanently incorporated into the teacher repertoire of behaviors, unless some other components are added. Figure 5-3 illustrates these components, some of which are discussed below.

(1) Presenters Who Can Model Effective Teaching Practices. This component is most important for presenters who are teaching pedagogy. Subject matter presentaters usually enjoy an audience which is motivated by the subject matter. As a result, the audience tends to be forgiving of poor teaching if subject expertise is evident. It is unforgivable, however, for these presenters to teach effective teaching practices in a manner that belies what is taught. Such practice exemplifies the old "do what I say, not what I do" technique.

Presenters who fail to perceive the relationship between effective practices and those which they personally model eventually lose credibility with teachers. Good modeling keeps the staff development effort afloat from the beginning.

(2) Demonstrating Learned Behaviors on Subject Matter. In Chapter 4, a method was given for teaching the professional practices which might be included in an evaluation system. A very strong component of this method is to make the teachers learners. Demonstrating learned behavior is, perhaps, the best way to reinforce the behavior. It is not uncommon to hear, "I didn't learn the material really well until I had to teach it." Demonstration is a method utilized to get the learner to internalize the behaviors or subject matter learned.

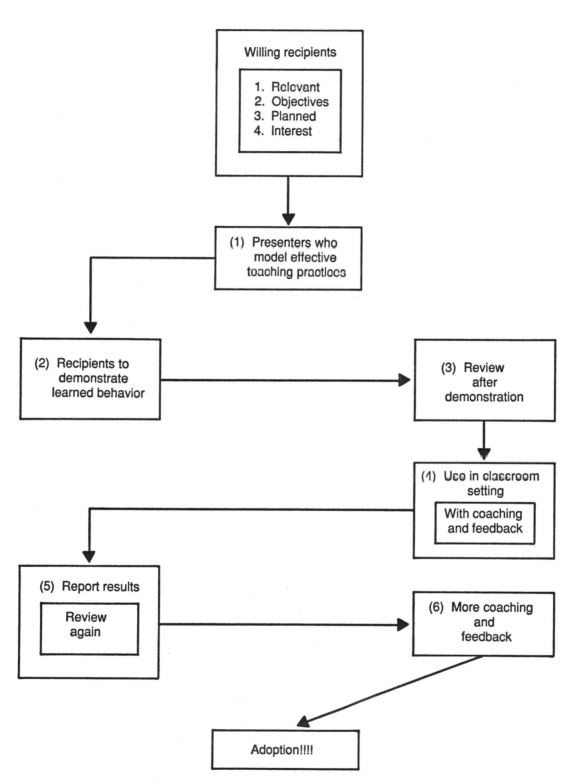

Figure 5-3 Producing Change with Staff Development.

There are other creative ways to demonstrate that which is learned. Some appropriate methods include the use of learning teams, with members demonstrating for each other and offering critiques. Another way for learners to demonstrate mastery is through the use of formative tests.

(3) Review. After use of any new concept, there are usually questions and comments. This is the time for review. Of course, review is most effective when it is cumulative and is conducted in an atmosphere that encourages free discussion. Cumulative review means that facts are added to a hierarchy, as the review progresses. For example, if there are five points to review, Point One is listed and discussed; then, Point One plus Point Two. Each time, the points discussed are listed, and a new point is added, until all five are completed. This method of review is quite effective in helping the learner to "set" the learned material mentally.

(4) Use in Classroom. This step requires coaching and feedback. Peers using videotapes, supervisors, or additional classroom visits may provide the teacher with the coaching that he or she needs. Trust is an important ingredient in coaching. The person who does the coaching and gives the feedback must realize that the learner is vulnerable and needs reinforcement more than anything else. The use of videotape in coaching will be discussed as a separate topic below.

(5) Report and Review Again. It is important that the group meet after initial trial of learned behavior in the classroom. Some members will have questions to share with the group, some will have reinforcing stories to tell, and it will become apparent that others will not have understood the material fully. This should lead to an opportunity for (1) support and commitment from the group, and (2) another review to clarify material not understood.

(6) Use with More Coaching and Feedback. At this stage, an additional attempt is made to use the newly learned material or behavior. Additional coaching should be provided. The coaching component is necessary and may be provided through a number of ways, such as by others who teach the new material, or by peers and supervisors.

Behavior adoption will only be achieved if the learner experiences success. Remember, most staff development is directed toward trying to change operational philosophy first. As previously points out however, change is likely to occur only after a "pay off" is observed.

The Use of Video Tape

Any discussion of coaching as an essential element of staff development should include some consideration of the use of the video camera in the classroom. Most schools have access to video cameras and recorders. It is relatively easy to set up a camera in the classroom, and the teacher can maintain control of the recorded tape. Coaching with videotape can begin with self-coaching.

Self-coaching is a process in which a teacher who has acquired new methods or behaviors can observe these skills his or her classroom when they are actually tried. The teacher can make judgments about the validity of the activity and how changes needed. There are several advantages to using video tape for coaching and even reinforcement. Some advantages are the following ones:

1. Self-coaching provides a view of one's performance in privacy and in an atmosphere that does not heighten ego involvement.
2. Peers can help, and they do not have to be physically present when the lesson is taught.
3. The teacher probably develops a more objective view of actual performance than with any other means.
4. The teacher can control the tape.
5. Improvement can be documented by multitapings.

Some disadvantages for taping include the following:

1. It is distracting to have the taping apparatus in the classroom.
2. It is difficult to set up the tape so that the teacher and the class can be viewed at the same time.
3. It takes quite a bit of self-confidence for the teacher to agree to be taped and to participate in an assessment and coaching.
4. A Teacher may not have the inclination or time to set up the equipment; thus, a second person must be involved.

Most of the disadvantages with the videotape can be overcome. The concept of self-coaching is particularly useful when teachers first begin to work with videotape. In a self-coaching arrangement, a camera and recorder are turned on at the beginning of a class. When the class activity is concluded, the teacher turns off the camera and retains the tape. At leisure, the teacher views the tape and then meets with a mentor to discuss what was observed and possible plans or actions for future lessons. The concept of using a mentor who does not actually view the tape is a way to force the teacher to make an analysis of the tape. The process of having the teacher discuss impressions with another person becomes a learning experience. Self-coaching is a valuable tool for getting acclimated to videotaping.

A LONG-TERM COMMITMENT

A commonly observed example of the need to change behaviors, experience success, and finally to change philosophy can be observed in the brief analysis of what typically occurs in the secondary school.

Secondary schools become hard core institutions. They have their own informal power structure and a complete set of cultural values. Secondary schools are so difficult to change that some educators claim, in jest, that it can't be done. Even though this claim is not taken seriously, there is a realization that it carries an element of truth.

Probably a wish of every superintendent is that high schools would more closely resemble elementary schools from the prospective of child centeredness. There is a desire that secondary teachers perceive students in a positive manner, that the needs of the student be placed above the institution, and that the summative mentality with which secondary students are taught would be lessened.

Staff development programs are devised to help create a humanistic climate. Some of the efforts include teacher effectiveness training, human relations in the classroom, mastery learning, etc. When John Goodlad* surveyed the American secondary school, he found procedures in the classrooms were virtually the same in every school observed. One might ask, "What, then, is the cost effectiveness for all the funds expended for staff development."

Possibly, if staff development is approached with the kind of practice and coaching advocated in Figure 5-3, and if the goal of experiencing success is provided prior to any concern about operational philosophy, the record of change resulting from staff development might not be as dismal.

Time

Change is a process that is somewhat slow. He or she who wishes to obtain a change of behavior in other human beings must be patient and tenacious. The review, coaching, and reinforcement must be spaced in a logically planned manner. For learning to stick, a review must be conducted shortly after learning. Even in the coaching and application stages, reviews must be periodically conducted as learning progresses. The time between reviews may be spaced at longer intervals, and the coaching and feedback can also be conducted at increasing intervals.

The time required for following the sequence outlined in Figure 5-3 could be a semester, a year, or even several years. There is a tendency for human beings to revert to old ways. This is particularly true if the old ways are easier or require less initial effort. Regression will occur even if the previous behaviors were ineffective. It is important to be certain that coaching and reinforcement are conducted.

The element of time is the reason that a school or school system should design a central focus and bring resources to bear on this focus. This can only be accomplished if the curriculum delivery system outlined in Figure 5-1 is tied together. Evaluation supported by staff development and staff development reinforced by evaluation is the symbiotic relationship that will facilitate change.

* John Goodlad. *A Place Called School.* New York: McGraw-Hill, 1983.

STAFF DEVELOPMENT AND THE STATE

With all the discussion of school reform, there are signs that the state will be assuming a greater role in the area of staff development. Most consequences of such a move will be detrimental because bureaucracies are usually ineffective in any endeavor which requires change. This is particularly true if the changes sought involve the way persons react or behave and changes in the operational philosophies they use. If bureaucracies are ever effective, it is in their allocation of resources and their establishment of mandatory compliance requirements.

Support with resources for staff development and mandatory program requirements, in a broad sense, are possibly, the only productive avenues open to the state. However, it must be recognized that the thrust of the current reform movement is the centralization of power, which is the antithesis to what effective school research would recommend.

A bureaucracy must have the means to monitor compliance. This raises the question, "How does one monitor compliance of attitude, philosophy, and belief system?" An attempt to reduce staff development to an auditing entity would be nonproductive. It is our view that the state role, as it relates to staff development, should be a limited one.

This is not to imply that the state should have no role in staff development. The end product of staff development—the monitoring of student outcomes—could be effectively evaluated by the state. If the state adopts this limited role, it will not become entangled in staff development processes. The state will allow staff development to be accomplished in an unencumbered manner, yet it still will review the end product of staff development.

THE CONTINUING BATTLE

It has been stated that staff development should involve pedagogical skills and content information. However, there is another area which should be addressed because it will be a part of any staff development consideration for the next decade. This involves the treatment of students. It is well documented that there are ways of treating students which will reduce the number of those who become disaffected, alienated, and make the decision that school is not the place to spend their time. Glasser* estimates that disaffected students exceed half the school population. Others who have studied the schools, particularly from the middle- and secondary-school perspective, agree with this analysis.

Disaffected students are those who no longer care about learning. Basically, they have decided that their needs cannot be met by trying to achieve as educators

---

* William Glasser, M.D. *Control Theory in the Classroom.* New York: Perennial Library, Harper and Row, 1986.

would have them do. They elect other ways for need fulfillment which are, at best, nonproductive, and, at worst, destructive.

Teachers typically react to these students with concern and, then, with hostility. The classroom becomes a battleground, and a continuing war is conducted. All of this occurs in the name of student motivation. These nonachievers are subjected to various motivational techniques, such as threats, embarrassment, failure, and intimidation.

The typical reader may question the existence of these negative motivational practices, but needs to look at some specific practices—giving "pop" quizzes; posting grades in public view; intentionally calling on students who do not know the answers; giving summative grades for homework; homogeneously grouping the "slow ones"; and projecting low expectancies for those who are not "bright."

This war, which is conducted with more than half the students, must be stopped. In reality, the country can no longer afford to have dysfunctional students merely find employment in some of the unskilled areas of heavy manufacturing and agriculture. This refuge will not be available to the next generation.

A discussion of some of the factors related to the so-called "war" in the classroom is not an implied indictment of teachers or of public education. At the least, the situation would be as bad or worse in private schools if all factors of student diversity were equal. The point is that all educators must make some very basic changes in how human beings are to work with others.

In this book, the stress has been placed on the motivational approach to evaluating teachers. When administrators and policy makers begin to work with teachers in a manner in which trust is exhibited, they encourage individual growth and expertise. In this atmosphere, the time will be "right" to help the teachers adopt new ways of working with students.

The disaffected student and the undeclared war which prevails as a standard operating procedure must become an area of staff development. In fact, this issue is of such overriding importance that it might be considered as an area for school or school system focus. To help teachers make the classroom a place where *all* students find success must be an agenda for staff development for many years to come.

SUMMARY

Figure 5-4 illustrates the close connection between staff development and evaluation of teaching performance. These two areas of the curriculum delivery system must be more closely connected than any of the components. Of course, as this chapter was developed, it was impossible to avoid returning often to the central focus. The idea of bringing all the professional and financial resources of a school system to a central focus is quite basic. The amazing thing, however, is that very few school systems marshall the best thinking available, decide upon a focus, and then coordinate the enormous resources available to cause "things to happen."

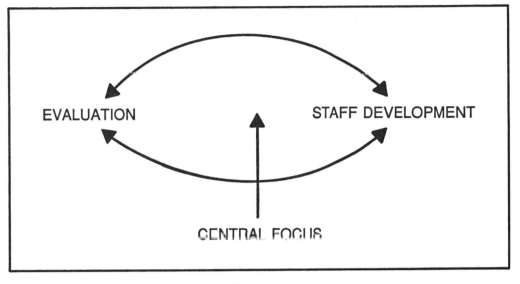

Figure 5-4

The importance of involving everyone in staff development can easily be recognized if we recall that about half of a school system's employees are members of the support staff. In most communities, support staff personnel are frequently active participants in churches, clubs, and other service organizations. This is especially true in school systems located in moderate population areas of the United States. (The majority of school systems enroll less than 10,000 students.) Staff development activities must be organized for everyone. It is desirable that staff personnel have a basic concept of how the professional personnel are to be evaluated.

Short-term, single-presentation staff development efforts usually do not work. For change to occur, the following efforts must be in place:

1. Appropriate modeling
2. Learner demonstration
3. Review
4. Application—coaching and review
5. More application and review
6. Coaching and feedback with further use
7. Time

Item seven is particularly important, since many Americans seem to emphasize short-term goals. If real change is to be achieved however, the long-term approach must be considered. The goal is to outlast the "nay sayers," the skeptics, "those who can't and those who won't," and those who have the tendency to revert to an old, comfortable nonproductive way of doing things. The positive use of time takes commitment.

The desired role for the state should be a supportive one. Perhaps, the state could monitor the end product of staff development. For the state to become involved in making prescriptions for staff development, and with subsequent compliance monitoring that accompanies bureaucratic effort, would possibly be a disastrous thing.

Finally, the great problem of the disaffected learner will have an overriding influence within the next decade. Finding a solution will involve evaluation, staff development, system focus, and all the other components of the curriculum delivery system. The educator with foresight will wish to look now at a comprehensive approach to working with this problem.

chapter 6

CONFERENCING AND SETTING PERFORMANCE TARGETS

The primary tool of evaluation is the conference, which is used to communicate the substance of evaluation. Whatever the purposes of evaluation, there is little chance for its accomplishment without skilled conferencing.

It is true that conferencing is a type of communication, but it is different from typical communication in that it involves more than being understood. Conferencing implies meeting for clearly defined purposes, with the meeting conducted in a structured environment, and with an agenda of specific activities to be covered.

The conferencing which precedes evaluation must support evaluation by reinforcing its purposes. In other words, the conferencing process must be consistent with the purposes of evaluation in every respect.

In the following pages, some different types of conferences will be discussed. Some of the most important "do's and don'ts" of evaluation conferences will be stressed, and the often omitted "follow-up conference" will receive special attention.

DETERMINING THE PURPOSES—A NECESSARY FIRST STEP

An old cliche is the following: "If you do not know where you are going, then how will you know when you arrive there?" This is true of conferencing. Each type of conference has its own separate set of purposes.

The different types of evaluation conferences are listed as follows:

1. Preconferences
2. Postconferences
3. Goal-setting conferences
4. Confrontational conferences
5. Follow-up conferences

Figure 6-1 shows how the conference types fit together to form a total approach for conferencing. Of course, there is some overlapping; techniques are seldom as clear-cut. However, unless purposes are clear, little will be accomplished.

Each of these evaluation conferences has specific utility. Preconferences and postconferences are often used with formative evaluation, whereas goal setting conferences and confrontational conferences are often used with summative evaluation. Of course, follow-up conferences are used with both summative and formative evaluations. The following text briefly describes the use of each type of conference.

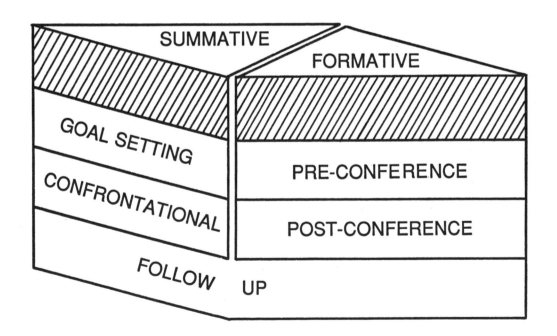

Figure 6-1 The Types of Conferences.

The Preconference

The preconference is a useful tool to set the stage for evaluation. The evaluator and the evaluatee can use the preconference to be certain that both parties clearly understand what is about to take place in an ensuing observation. An extremely important task associated with the preconference is for the evaluator to identify what he or she will be expecting to see (i.e., certain performance indicators or teaching behaviors), and for the evaluatee to describe his or her teaching plan for the class session.

It is important that both parties understand the teacher's plans for class on the day of observation. From these plans, the evaluator may decide that he or she will not have a chance to see several aspects of teaching demonstrated. In this case, it is better for the evaluator to schedule the observation for another day. For example, a teacher may plan to test the students or to have a guest speaker.

Other purposes of the preconference are the following:

1. To create a relaxed atmosphere
2. To learn about the unique qualities of the class
3. To hear about student outcomes that are sought
4. For the observer to explain precisely what performance indicators he or she will focus upon
5. To establish procedures in advance—where the evaluator will sit, what will be written, how much time will be spent on observation, and when feedback will be given

The most important aspect of the preconference is to develop a collegial atmosphere that is free of anxiety and threat before the observation takes place. To hear about student outcomes is important, because this emphasis reinforces the goal of preset outcomes as a basic component of teaching. When evaluators first began to ask about outcomes, answers similar to the following were not atypical: "We will read . . . and discuss it"; or, "We plan to finish Chapter 6 and then answer the questions." Of course, to "read about and discuss" is not an outcome. These examples demonstrate why discussing student outcomes is critical. In fact, the evaluator may have to give some in-service on teaching to outcomes.

The Postconference

Of course, the postconference is conducted after the observation. In the postconference, the observer conveys what he or she saw during the observation. It will help communication if the observer does not have to relate the "good" and "bad" things observed.

This gets back to an important question: "How can a person improve if he or she is not told what is wrong?" On occasion, it is appropriate for the observer to tell what was done wrong or what factors impeded instruction. This approach must be handled carefully so that the "good news / bad news" syndrome can be avoided. Identifying problems can easily destroy observer/teacher relationships so this approach is recommended only as a last resort, or when the existing relationship is so positive and the teacher ego so solid that damage will not be likely to occur.

A word of caution is appropriate here. There is an inclination for each administrator to believe that he or she has a unique ability to offer positive criticism and get results or change. Don't believe it! "Positive criticism" is, perhaps, the most notorious oxymoron used in teaching.

There are two occasions when the "bad news" must be given: (a) when the teacher does not realize that what he or she is doing is ineffective; and (b) when a teacher engages in a practice which hurts students or violates policy. As can be seen, the first problem results mainly from a problem of perception. The second problem arises from a myriad of causes. Although causes are important, it is usually first necessary to extinguish the behavior immediately. Then the determination of cause can be analyzed. It may be necessary to employ the confrontational conference for both these occasions.

As previously discussed, a formative observation from a positive protocol is desired. In such a situation, the preconference is used to identify a specific list of teaching skills to be observed. In the postconference, each skill is listed, and teaching actions which fit each skill are noted. A skill with a no response indicates that nothing which applied to that skill was observed. It does not take a genius to parley this situation into several avenues of assistance and reach consensus about what might be done.

Postconferences are for feedback. They are usually implemented as part of formative evaluation. Change is the goal of formative evaluation, and change occurs only in a healthy climate. The ego must be protected, and a feeling of self-worth must be preserved. A novice cannot do these things well, but skills can be taught that will enable observers to receive requests for assistance in problem areas from the observed. Additional information given later in this chapter will be helpful in identifying some of these skills.

Finally, a postconference is not a "tell it like it is" session. It is an indisputable fact that a relationship can be "shut down" quickly and easily if sensitivity is not practiced. The heightened use of rationalization is the first hint given to the observer to proceed with care. In fact, the use of any defense mechanism frequently indicates that the focus of the postconference has changed. Once this happens, the probability is that the conferee will not hear or objectively interpret further input. At this point, the evaluator has the option of trying to re-establish the climate of understanding or of abandoning the process until a "restart" can be initiated. This view may seem extreme. It is true, however, that once the teacher becomes threatened, little, if anything, can be accomplished.

The Goal-Setting Conference

Occasionally in a formative, and frequently in a summative situation, it is desirable to conduct a goal-setting conference. One would normally assume that goal setting should be a part of any conference, and this is true to some extent. In a formative mode however, the goal setting is informal and flows naturally as a part of the postconference.

When a special conference is created to set performance targets or goals, the need for targets is usually established from a summative evaluation. In other words, performance has been evaluated, needs have been identified, and targets have been set around these needs. This is a simple and straightforward process, but it is only marginally effective. It will achieve compliance or minimum standards, but has little utility for long-term change.

A conference to set performance targets should contain the following elements:

1. A precise description of the performance desired
2. A description of the teacher and the observer roles in providing perquisites and assistance prior to the expected accomplishment of the target
3. A plan for demonstration of the target, details of how it is to be observed, standards for satisfactory performance, and projected time lines

The Confrontational Conference

There are times when a behavior or practice must be changed immediately. For example, a teacher may be engaging in a practice which is disruptive to the school or harmful to students. In such a case, the immediacy of the situation may not allow for subtle ego-saving approaches.

The confrontational conference needs to be brief and descriptive. The problem effect and why its existence is unacceptable must be explained. A later time must be set to review progress. The following example involves an employee who has been arriving late for work frequently.

> *The Problem—* "You were late twice this week and twice last week."

Its Effect—	"This is a real problem for me, and I need your help. I am concerned. All teachers need to be at their classroom door before bell time.
Why Unacceptable—	"Each person is expected to uphold this goal."
Follow-Up Plan—	"I know you can help me with this. I will follow-up with you in ten days—that is, on the first of June."

Notice that the confronter did not use an accusing or condemning approach. After a statement of fact, the confronter did not focus on the person with the problem, but upon his own reaction to the problem, his thinking about it.

A confronter who uses this approach will probably get through the first three stages before the perpetrator responds. However, just before the follow-up stage, the teacher or perpetrator is likely to respond in one of the following ways: "One of those days, I was not late. But, I do remember having some very unusual problems last week"; or, "Our baby sitter quit, and I had to drive . . ."

At this point, the confronter should focus on the purpose of the confrontation. He or she should use a polite and positive tone. Examples follow: "I understand what you are saying—unusual things happen" ; "Let's set a follow-up conference for ten days from now—that's June 1"; "Let's look at the situation then."

Some guidelines for confrontational conferences are as follows:

1. Don't accuse or demean.
2. Don't project hostility.
3. Don't accept the problem or become sidetracked.
4. Focus attention away from the person and onto the problem.

The Follow-up Conference

The follow-up conference is the most frequently omitted conference. It is the necessary component of a two-part procedure—the initial conference and the follow-up. The only conference type which does not require a follow-up conference is the preconference.

The reasons for omitting the follow-up conference are organizational and psychological. The follow-up conference practically doubles the effort needed to address most problems. Scheduling is required, and plans for the conference must be made. It is easier to assume closure after the initial conference.

From the psychological perspective, it is often difficult for the initiator of the conference to go through the potential hostility, disagreement, and tenseness of talking about someone's performance. When the initial conference is complete, there is a tendency to relax and feel relieved that it is over. A follow-up conference is perceived as having to "bring up" the problem again.

The purposes of a follow-up conference are as follows:

1. To set a time for future accountability
2. To provide positive feedback if the problem has been remediated or if any improvement has been noted
3. To plan further if the problem continues
4. To give structure to the entire process of conferencing
5. To attend to a relationship which may have cooled because of interactions of the first conference

IMPROVE CONFERENCE SKILLS AND IMPROVE EVALUATION

The lack of appropriate conferencing skills is the primary reason that practically all teachers in all schools get high ratings. If one believes that the normal curve of distribution is even slightly applicable to teachers, it can be assumed that one-half the population should fall below average. Even if evaluators skew the results, certainly eighty percent of the population could not be performing in the top ten percent. However, this mathematical paradox commonly occurs with teacher evaluation.

Most principals have reached an accommodation with teacher evaluations. Principals are accorded respect as they go about their duties of evaluating, and they give most teachers excellent ratings. When questioned by outsiders (not by their own superintendents), principals will candidly state that the hostility that they will engender if they act otherwise is not worth the trouble. Others say that high morale in a school is important for production and that the central office judges poor morale as a *lack of leadership ability*. So, why risk creating morale problems by giving teachers realistic evaluations?

Honest evaluations do not have to create morale problems. Other than the quality of the evaluation system, the improvement of conferencing skills offers the greatest promise for improving teaching and obtaining realistic evaluation results. Productive conferences cannot be conducted if inhibitors interfere. Some of the most common inhibitors for purposeful conferences are:

1. Self-interest
2. Personal actions

Each of these qualities, and some of the attributes needed for successful communication, will be discussed next.

Self-interest

Figure 6-2 illustrates how self must be sublimated in order for purposes to be clearly addressed in a conference. Needs, emotions, and attitude are isolated; and the focus of the conference can then be directed toward procedures leading to success.

If the initiator of a conference is unable to extract self from the proceedings, he or she ends up with personal needs, emotions, and attitudes entangled in the conference procedure. This attitude distracts from the purpose of the conference, can be annoying, and can possibly confuse the teacher.

Admittedly, the prospect of the administrator removing self from the conference is not very promising. This requires more training in conferencing than is normally available in evaluator training programs. A helpful exercise is for the administrator to become acquainted with self prior to a conference. This mental exercise appears to help bring thoughts and feelings to the surface. Prior contemplation helps to get emotions and attitudes under control. Four questions, useful for self-analysis and which should be asked before a conference begins, are listed in Figure 6-3.

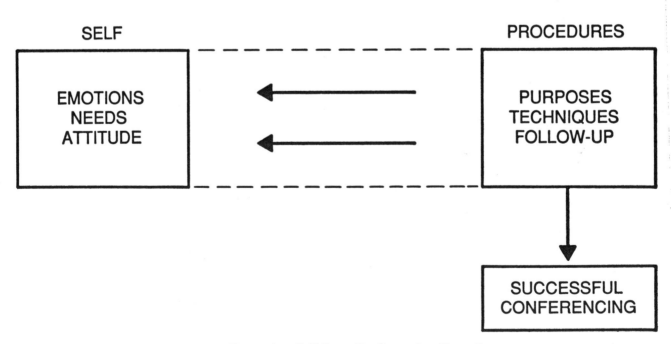

Figure 6-2 Removing Self from Conferencing Procedures.

Self-Analysis Before a Conference

1. What is my attitude about this conference? (Write ten words or less.)_____

   _____

   _____

2. List one to three personal concerns:

   a._____

   _____

   b._____

   _____

   c._____

   _____

3. How do I want to be perceived? (Write ten words or less.)_____

   _____

   _____

4. What aspects of this conference are emotionally charged? (Write ten words or less.)_____

   _____

   _____

Figure 6-3

With a little practice, administrators can use the questions posed in Figure 6-3 as a basis to dissect their personal feelings (self) before directing a conference. By bringing these needs, attitudes, and emotions to the open, they are less likely to have these feelings emerge as handicaps in the conference. For example, let's look at one of the questions and how self-analysis could be used. Suppose that a confrontational conference has been scheduled and plans have been made to address a serious problem. The need to sublimate self in favor of accomplishing the purposes of the conference has been realized, and the self-analysis exercise is initiated.

Question 1.—   What is my attitude about this conference?
Answer—   I'm offended by this person and personally insulted by his action.

Possible answers to this question may illustrate its functional value. If the feelings expressed were allowed to remain at a semiconscious level and emerged at the conference, the accomplishment of purpose could be lost. By initiating self-analysis and bringing the feelings into the open, the administrator has a better chance of exerting self-control and attending to the real purpose of the conference.

Notice that "I and my" were used in two of the questions in the self-analysis. It is desirable to unload all of the "I's" and "my's" before any conference begins. The focus should be on the person being evaluated at the conference. To have the administrator lapse into using just a few "I and my" statements could distract from the purpose of the conference. The extensive use of "I" and "my" will cause the administrator to lose credibility as a caring person who is interested in others.

Personal Actions

During the conference, the personal actions of the initiator either contribute or detract from the conference. Conference success may depend more on skills used than on actual content.

It is important to create an atmosphere of acceptance, and seven positive actions that can build this atmosphere are the following:

1. Move from behind the desk.
2. Sit in an open, relaxed position—without hands, arms, or legs crossed—but not in a slouched position.
3. Don't shake or tighten vocal cords. Trembling hands and changes in speech patterns convey a message of anxiety, and this threatens some conferees.
4. Initiate small talk to set atmosphere: for example, ask a question about

a small personal observation. The purpose of small talk is to give recognition to the other person that he or she is important.

5. Summarize the other person's position.
6. Don't be afraid to show that you have given thought to the conference thought: for example, "I was thinking about how we might approach this last night."
7. End with a positive tone, if possible.

Seven actions which serve to make a conference ineffective are the following:

1. Have ready solutions available.
2. Attempt to appear competent or in control.
3. Use implied threats.
4. Try to embarrass the other person into complying.
5. Look at your watch at least five times.
6. Read or stare out the window while the other person is talking.
7. Demonstrate that you are uncomfortable with having to deal with trivia.

The most effective tool of the conference is the smile. An evaluator who cannot find at least two things to smile about in a classroom observation period is taking him- or herself too seriously. Identify the light things, and mention them in the conference. This practice puts the teacher at ease. It also gives the evaluator something to smile about and credibility as a "regular" person.

It is difficult for people who do not have reasonably positive self-concepts to be accepting of others. This deficit, in turn, makes productive conferencing very difficult to achieve. Those who have reached adulthood without a positive view of life may require more nurturing than either time or training will allow for them to become effective at conferencing. For these individuals, personal needs will preclude their being able to sublimate self in order to meet the needs of others. For this reason, it is recommended that evaluators be chosen from those who already possess the basic personal prerequisities of self-confidence and who are ready to accept others as persons of value.

Directed Discovery

The positive protocol is made effective through the technique of "directed discovery." This technique usually works in ways similar to the following:

Teacher A:	"You were looking for examples of eight performance indicators. How did I do?"
Observer B:	"Great, let me tell you what I saw . . ."
Teacher C:	"You didn't mention Number Eight."
Observer D:	"I didn't observe it. Maybe I missed something. Let me tell you what I look for here . . ."
Teacher E:	"Who can I observe who is good at that?"
Observer F:	"Mrs. Jamerson, next door. I'll help set it up."

This same situation could take many turns. For example, the teacher may contend that the observer missed something. This need not be a problem. Just schedule another visit for the specific purpose of observing the missed performance indicator. Remember that the goal is to strengthen performance through a positive approach.

Other problems also require the use of directed discovery. For example, a teacher may just passively accept the evaluator's assessment. This reaction needs to be changed since the observer or evaluator has no way of knowing the teacher's real feelings. Therefore, the observer must initiate action in order to obtain closure. The observer may choose to take some of the responsibility for possibly not observing the behavior: "I missed Number Eight . . . . Let me tell you what's involved in demonstrating this competency."

Directed discovery is a means of accomplishing purpose. It is much more effective than criticism, because it keeps the focus on the desired performance and not on the individual.

THE PRICE OF FAILURE

A successful evaluative conference either sets the stage for improvement and growth or, as with confrontational conferences, for the resolution of a problem. If these positive results are not achieved, the resulting failure has some rather serious consequences that include the following:

1. Stress and its debilitating effect on individuals
2. Conflict with time and energy devoted to doing battle
3. Third-party combatants which entangles the organization
4. Sanctions, whereby each side withholds something of value from the other.

In an organization where the effects of stress, conflict, or sanctions are manifest, the consequences do not only involve the combatant parties. Usually, third-party combatants are also involved in the conflict. An astute administrator once observed, "In education, we could go to jail and employ three felons. If, within three weeks, these felons commit felonious actions at work, each could nonetheless produce ten fellow workers who would testify to their innocence."

Even thought this observation is extreme, it points to the fact of inevitable third-party involvement. With third-party involvement, discontent can spread through the entire staff. With a broad base of involvement, the conflict can quickly escalate to the use of sanctions. The administrator may withhold giving institutional rewards. For example, "From this point, anyone who requests to leave early because personal emergencies will have his or her pay docked." In retaliation, the teachers may announce, "We will only do the minimum work required by the contract."

Ineffective conferencing tends to destroy most benefits of evaluation. Of course, if conferencing skills are lacking, the effect will be felt in other parts of the school environment. Effective conferencing can help avoid conflicts similar to the one that has been outlined above.

SUMMARY

The conference is identified as the primary tool of evaluation. Adequate conferencing skills keep very threatening situations from becoming disruptive and nonproductive.

The determination of purpose, as well as the keeping of it in the forefront, is critical. Purpose is enforced through selection of the type of conference to initiate. Some ways to keep the conference on target are these:

1. Set a relaxed atmosphere.
2. Protect the ego of the other person.
3. Avoid ready-made solutions.
4. Do not accept responsibility for the problem or the desired change.
5. Do not get sidetracked with unrelated discussions.
6. Restate the intended outcomes, and set a follow-up conference.

The confrontational conference is particularly difficult for some administrators, because it has the potential to engender hostile relationships and can lead to both participants invoking sanctions Some suggestions for effective confrontational conferences include identifying the problem, telling its effect, exploring why the present situations are unacceptable, and setting a follow-up.

It was mentioned earlier that teacher evaluation is often an exercise which is debilitating to the teacher's morale. This result is partly attributable to the use of "good news / bad news" approach to conferencing. The "good news/bad news" approach should only be used in summative evaluations, and then only in confrontational conferences when a "stop it" message must be given. Even in confrontational conferences, the skills listed within this chapter will help reduce long-range negative effects.

Criticism is identified as always negative in consequence. For this reason, criticism is not recommended for the formative evaluation. To abandon criticism requires skill. If criticism is not used, the evaluator must be able to lead the teacher to identify the appropriate concerns. With practice, "directed discovery" is not overly difficult to implement.

The follow-up conference is identified as necessary. It serves as a means of interjecting an element of accountability into any conference situation. The follow-up conference is set mainly for the conferee to know that the conference topics will be re-examined within a specific time.

Removing self from the conference is critical for its success. The administrator must be able to isolate his or her emotional reactions and keep them from interfering with the purposes of the conference.

Finally, failure to succeed in conferencing leads to stress and conflict. Of course, this is counterproductive for any evaluation.

chapter 7

EVALUATION AS A TERMINAL ACTIVITY

The information contained in this chapter is different from those that preceded or which follow. These other chapters were designed to assist the administrator to avoid "terminal activity." However, despite all efforts, there are those who remain incompetent or who otherwise create "cause" for termination. The administrator must then move the evaluative process from the formative to the summative realm. The difference in approach that is dictated by this move was discussed in Chapter 1, which stated the purpose of a summative evaluation is one of summary. The primary questions become whether or not job targets have been accomplished and whether there is a reasonable expectancy that they may be accomplished. In a summative assessment, the results of performance are summarized. If the negative impact of poor performance is significant, a change must occur rapidly. Otherwise, continuance of the employment relationship must be altered or must cease.

PREPARING TO WIN

Reasons which create cause for termination are included in state statutes. Such reasons usually include incompetence, immorality, violation of school board policy, and conviction of a felony. Basically, the same preparation, due process and documentation, is required for most statutorily permissible reasons for termination. Therefore, rather than discuss all causes for termination, incompetency will be used, in a comprehensive sense, throughout this chapter. Incompetency is the most frequently cited reason for teacher termination, and its existence is one of the problems of public education most frequently cited by the popular press.

With a decision to consider the termination of employment, concern for improvement of performance remains, but the term "winning" takes on new meaning. To "win" means a better learning experience for students. To "lose" has devastating consequences. It means that incompetent performance may continue or that resources will be expended with no resulting benefit for the students. This chapter will contain guidelines on preparing to win. Figure 7-1 outlines some of the strategies for winning which will be discussed in this chapter.

> *Obtaining improvement is the goal, but winning in efforts to remove incompetence becomes critical. A no-risk win is to terminate problem without terminating employment.*

THE NO-RISK WIN

Of course, it is well known that there is very little possibility of "no risk" when working with performance, but a most acceptable win is to secure competent performance or a resignation, thereby avoiding dismissal and possible court action. This win can be accomplished by the following means: (1) making a final effort to assist the teacher; (2) reassigning the teacher; or (3) preparing for dismissal in such a thorough manner that a resignation is tendered. If these efforts do not succeed, then the fact that efforts were made prepares the stage for the most expensive and time-consuming win—termination or dismissal.

Making the Final Effort

Prior to bringing continuation of the employment relationship into question, it is assumed that performance targets were set in accordance to goal-setting and conferencing procedures similar to those outlined in Chapter 6, but that performance continued to be unsatisfactory. This is the time for drastic action, which can also be an innovative action in the form of a "final effort" approach. This is likely to be costly, but less expensive than the cost of hearings or litigation. The final effort may include the following: soliciting cooperation of the union or teacher association; the assignment of a cooperative teacher from existing staff; or the employment of a substitute teacher, such as a recently retired teacher, to work with the class while assistance is given to the incompetent teacher. The possible solutions for the final effort are restricted only by the imagination. One example of a final effort is given on the next page.

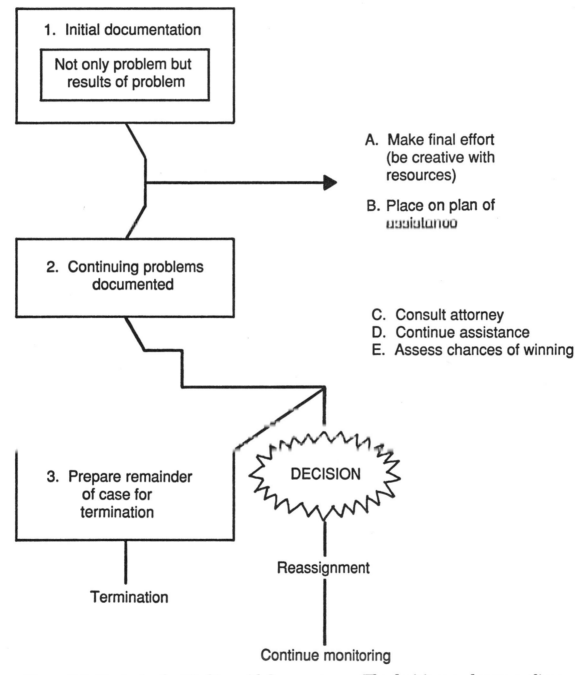

Figure 7-1 Strategies for Working with Incompetence. (The decisions and steps outlines might encompass a year or two, and each step taken is based upon the failure of the previous step.)

A new teacher was having difficulty in organizing her class of primary children into routines, whereby the classroom would be in the teacher's control. Prior to employment, the teacher was viewed by the principal as having great potential. She had an outstanding college career, which included successful student-teaching experience, and success in the classroom was anticipated. The problems with classroom routines were brought to the attention of central office supervision by a group of irate parents. By this time, the principal had practically exhausted his repertoire of ways to help. These efforts included diagnosis of the problem, conferences, tapes, books, supervision, and technical and organizational prescription. The parents threatened to remove their children from school and to protest the situation at a public school board meeting.

The time for a final effort had certainly arrived. An experienced teacher was brought into the classroom to establish routines and to get the class organized. The new teacher was removed and was accompanied by an experienced supervisor to observe some of the most competent teachers in the school system. In the observation process, the organizational techniques and the schedule of routines of the competent teachers were the main focus. After two days of observation with the supervisor and several additional days with the master teachers, the teacher was returned to her class. By this time, the class was well under control with the tutelage of the experienced teacher. The new teacher now assumed the role of aide to the experienced teacher. Slowly the teacher was phased from the role of aide to a leadership role, as the experienced teacher was phased out. The final result was a classroom with established routines and structure, and the experienced teacher was phased out completely.

The example given above is overly simplified. Certainly, an overnight transition did not occur. However, with frequent supervision, the classroom situation was brought to an acceptable level. The main point is that final efforts are comprehensive and that they involve personnel and commitment. They are usually more costly than the assistance which is ordinarily provided.

In addition to the possibility of assisting with improved performance, final efforts make an excellent source of documentation should dismissal proceedings become necessary. With documentation, it can be demonstrated clearly that an effort of exceptional magnitude was made to provide the incompetent teacher with assistance.

Reassigning the Teacher

One might ask, "How can the reassignment of an incompetent teacher be justified?" This is, indeed, a probing question; but, conversely, one might ask, "How can it be assumed that incompetence in one situation means incompetence in all situations?" It may be appropriate to use reassignment, such as in the following cases: (1) motives will be misinterpreted—termination is likely to be viewed as racially or politically motivated; (2) success in the dismissal proceedings is questionable; and (3) the resources of time and money for dismissal procedures are not available.

Motives Misinterpreted. If termination is likely to be misinterpreted by a significant constituency, the facts which must be addressed are not of documentable nature, but of perception. Perceived facts may or may not relate to reality. Perception has prevented educational progress and rendered moot the finest of plans. To act precipitously, and without a proper assessment of variables and all alternative ways of removing the incompetence, may be ill-advised, indeed. Of course, a wise administrator continues to strengthen the documentation in case the reassignment plan does not work.

Chances to Win Are Poor. Even though both the principal and others recognize a serious problem with a teacher's performance, it may not be prudent to move for dismissal. Caution could be precipitated by incomplete documentation or by actions taken by the teacher or others. Anything which significantly cuts the odds for winning in a dismissal case may make the process unacceptable. If an administrator sees a potential problem, this should be discussed with the school board attorney, the superintendent, or other appropriate person. An example of an action of the teacher or others that might have reduced the chances of winning is cited below:

> The administration became aware of incompetent performance as a result of the principal's observation. All the appropriate steps were followed by the principal, but improvement was insufficient. Supervisory assistance was obtained from the central office. Following other efforts to assist, the principal prepared to put the teacher on notice of impending termination. However, the teacher realized that the principal was "closing in" and made an attack at the administration by writing a letter to the local newspaper editor. The letter alleged a lack of support in assisting teachers with disciplinary problems and "turning the head" when students openly abused teachers. Within a few days of this letter, the teacher's picture appeared in the paper, together with a brief article that reported recognition by her college alumni for work on a scholarship committee.
>
> The principal and central administration had two new problems to face: (1) a potential charge of retaliation for exercise of free speech; and (2) a possible public relations problem with the community. This narrative underscores the necessity for the administration to approach the need for termination with a degree of flexibility and, perhaps, for the need to exercise other options, which may include consultation with a knowledgeable attorney at an early stage.

Time and Cost Too Great. An administrative unit can simultaneously engage in only a limited number of litigation or quasi-litigation (such as due process hearings) proceedings. A single dismissal, which proceeds through all appropriate hearings and through court to the U.S. district level, can cost thousands of dollars and require hundreds of man hours. Courts have little sympathy with work-strained loads, or the fact that other litigation is in progress. An attempt to regulate the work load by taking on only a limited number of cases at a time is advised. A failure to keep litigation at a reasonable level may result in other parts of the educational program being neglected.

Finally, if the possibilities of winning are viewed as limited, a try at another assignment for the incompetent teacher may be a worthy alternative. Of course, as with all final efforts, reassignment can afford additional possibilities for documentation and for demonstrating a genuine effort to assist the teacher.

Careful Preparation

The act of preparing for a termination has been observed to cause a change in the performance of the teacher, who may realize, for the first time, that his or her situation is, indeed, serious. In such preparation, the administrator is forced to ask, "Has every prudent and reasonable effort been made to secure competent performance?" This posed question may result in an additional effort. When a well-documented case is evident, attorneys and other third-party representatives are more anxious to seek face-saving solutions, such as voluntary resignation, than litigation.

Third-party representation may come from the teacher union or teachers' association. These organizations must approach termination cases in terms of economics and potential to win. If the documentation is well prepared, if a clear effort to assist the teacher to perform satisfactorily is evident, and if the applicable statutes have been followed meticulously, these groups tend to seek a negotiated solution. If a resignation is not negotiated, these third parties are unlikely to support an obvious loser past the first due process hearing. In either case, the removal of incompetence may be achieved at a reduced cost in terms of time and resources.

SUGGESTIONS FOR DOCUMENTING

When the decision is made that efforts to correct incompetent performance are not working and that continued incompetence cannot be tolerated, careful documentation is a must, and several items, such as the following, must be considered: (1) What should be documented?; (2) When should an attorney be consulted?;

(3) When should a microcomputer be used?; (4) How much documentation is enough?; (5) How should checklists and written evaluations be used?

What Should Be Documented?

The most important rule for documentation is thoroughness. Hearings, court cases, and perceptions of fairness all depend upon documentation. This process, then, must contain precise information. It must indicate specifically what was wrong with the teacher's performance, what was done to assist the teacher, and must also indicate that the teacher was fully informed as the process proceeded.

For some, documentation starts at the moment of employment: policies are reviewed or expectancy statements are given. For others, serious documentation does not begin until the teacher is officially informed of a problem and until the evaluation process has assumed a summative nature. Copious notes and records are the rule of documentation. For example, several informal efforts to help may have been made prior to the teacher's first official notification of a problem. Of course, records of such assistance should be available.

Witnesses should be present at all conferences where problems in performance are discussed and further expectancy statements given. Each witness should make a written summary of the meeting. The principal and all other administrators should retain copies of every piece of communication exchanged with the teacher. Even the appointment calendar can become important. A case in which this writer was involved possibly turned on the use of a two-year old appointment calendar which verified that a critical meeting was, indeed, conducted. Another detail which is sometimes omitted is a recording of the exact date on every document. A missing date may give rise to unnecessary legal haggling. The typical letter of documentation should include the following:

1. Date
2. Precise description of problem
3. Negative results of the problem
4. A description of the corrective action expected
5. A description of assistance which has been provided (if any) and a new plan of assistance—be sure to list only those forms of assistance which can be delivered
6. Date for an assessment of results

It is not atypical for three or four letters of documentation—with each letter outlining a new effort to help and the resulting expectancies—to be in a file. Each letter should be accompanied by the following: (1) notes of the conference, at which letter was given to the teacher; (2) observation reports; and (3) notes on the conference following observations. The number of documents may exceed thirty to forty pages by the time a due process hearing is held.

When an Attorney Is Consulted

The wise administrator involves an attorney early in the process—at least by the time the teacher is notified of a serious problem and the commencement of the summative evaluation. Possibly, the best guide for introduction of the attorney into the process is when the principal decides that improvement must be forthcoming if the employment relationship is to continue. It is noteworthy that school attorneys believe they are most effective when they are brought into the case early and before significant errors have been made.

When the attorney enters the scene, his responsibilities should include the following:

1. Reviewing existing records
2. Giving guidance about present potential to win
3. Giving guidance about how the case might be strengthened
4. Making sure that the administration complies with due process requirements, statutory requirements, and deadlines

An attorney's effectiveness can be enhanced by interpreting the educational significance of documented evidence for him or her. Most attorneys do not profess to be educators, and a close working relationship for interpretive purposes is advantageous. It is also helpful to organize the documentation in ways which make the sequence of events easy to follow and to have a written summary from all witnesses. It is important to remember that the attorney cannot help with a plan or prepare a case with information which is not on hand or with an assumed testimony.

A word about attorneys! Educational law has become such a specialized field of law that it is impossible for the general practitioner to be fully informed and up-to-date. This leaves the administrator with two choices: (1) to train a good general practitioner; or (2) to employ a specialist. In a rural area, some combination of the two may be the best solution.

How Much Documentation is Enough?

With the importance of thorough documentation stressed, there may be a tendency to document that which is both insignificant and petty. Documentation of petty occurrences is not a problem, unless such documentation is used in a hearing.

This will give rise to accusations of a predetermined bias which resulted in the development of insignificant evidence. It remains the best practice to document carefully; when dismissal charges are raised however, choose only the strongest and most significant documentation. For example, "failure to maintain discipline" is the primary cause of incompetence, then do not add "failure to report to work on time" to the charge, especially if only two or three instances of minor tardiness can be documented. Perhaps, "failure to be prepared for class" contributed to the lack of class discipline, with tardiness and other items as indications of a lack of preplanning. This evidence could be given in testimony. A concern for not "overcrowding" the significant items should be discussed with the school board attorney.

Use of Microcomputer

Documentation and paperwork in a dismissal proceeding can quickly escalate from thirty to forty pages to a few hundred pages. The task of managing paper and knowing who said what becomes a herculean task. This task can be made easier with any good file program and a microcomputer. All information can be reduced to a more manageable form by creating a file program which includes data, such as writer, date, subject, and a one-line summary. From this information, indexes can be generated, and data can be copied and organized into folders chronologically and according to subject and writer. During a hearing, such organization enables the attorneys to have, on hand, every memo about every subject sent or received by the witness giving testimony. Distracting fumbling through pages of papers is eliminated.

Checklist or Written Narrative

Checklists, as discussed in earlier chapters, are composed of lists of desirable characteristics for competent teaching. As stated in Chapter 1, the desired qualities listed may or may not relate to research-based characteristics of teaching which produce positive outcomes. The primary problems with checklists are that they are not precise and that they easily lead to incorrect assumptions about performance. Checklists usually contain a rating scale of one through five, with five being the most positive rating. The imprecise nature of a checklist may be highlighted by a question: What does a "three" rating mean for the characteristic, "lesson plans"? Perhaps, this means that the lesson plans were average. Then, one might ask: "What is an average lesson plan?" At any rate, these types of question engender legal debate, and the school system pays while the meter runs.

As checklists lead to incorrect assumptions, those completed in prior years tend to become exhibits for the teacher's defense. The focus of the problem is that principals who tend to give the teachers a "three" understand the unwritten code related to this rating—a three rating on a five-point scale sends a message of improvement needed. A rating of two is viewed as disastrous.

Even though the principal and teacher understand the unwritten code, such a rating may be interpreted in court to mean that performance was average. Certainly, this rating is not an appropriate documentation for termination.

Written evaluations are much preferred to checklists. To continue with the example of "lesson plans" which received a three, a written evaluation might read as follows: "lesson plans were prepared, but there was no statement of learning goals or outcomes." This states simply what was observed. Thus, misunderstanding is avoided. The problems with checklists are eliminated with the written narrative, but only if the evaluator avoids general terms and uses a precise description of what was observed.

HELPING THE ADMINISTRATOR

Once the documentation nears completion, last efforts have failed, and termination is sought, some training is in order for the administrators involved in providing testimony in the due-process hearings and court action. There are two potential psychological problems inherent in dismissal for the administrator.

In developing the documentation, the administrator tends to become involved in the case to the extent that he or she is likely to feel frustrated from the questions of friendly and hostile attorneys. It is difficult for the administrator to respond unemotionally to questions which appear to challenge the veracity of his or her assessment. Typical responses heard among administrators are the following: "Who is on trial here?"; "This is not worth it . . . This may be my last time."

A problem for administrators is that administrators are success-oriented. There is a general belief among school administrators that, with enough effort and skill, anything can be fixed. Accordingly, when termination is necessary, the administrator may experience feelings of failure or guilt.

Preparation for the psychological problem outlined above and for others can be accomplished by some staff development activities organized around topics, such as (1) the nature of cross-examination, (2) role playing, (3) a discussion of the result of failure to confront incompetence, and (4) discussion sessions designed to bring frustration to the surface. The goal is to emerge from the dismissal process with conscientious administrators who remain determined to continue to provide the best education for the students and to face necessary hardships, as required.

WHO ARE THE INCOMPETENT?

In thinking about evaluation as a terminal activity, you may begin to consider which teachers ought to be terminated. Of course, the building principal knows who the incompetent ones are. He is the first person, after the school custodian, who is likely to identify incompetence. In a serious vein, the best kept secret in education is the number of incompetent teachers in the system. The popular impression is that there are vast numbers of incompetent teachers within the schools. They are thought to be hiding under their grade books, in waste cans, and, of course, in the teacher's lounge. Actually, incompetence among members of the teaching profession is an anomaly. In most school systems, it is estimated that less than two percent of the teaching staff are incompetent.

In Chapter 1, the dual nature of the evaluation system was discussed. It was stated that educators often neglect the ninety-eight percent and waste excessive amounts of time with the two percent. As was pointed out, there must be two clearly different modes of evaluation—the formative mode for those with the greatest potential for improvement, and the summative mode for evaluation directed toward removing the incompetent. One problem is that the majority of the ninety-eight percent who are not incompetent are average. The public will accept average bricklayers and average attorneys, but has little tolerance for average teachers. Endeavors to enhance professional growth of those who are in the average range is where most of the administrator's time should be utilized.

DOCUMENTATION FOR E.E.O.C. COMPLAINTS

A complaint can be lodged with the Equal Employment Opportunity Commission (E.E.O.C.) for almost any job action which will vaguely support allegations of a discriminatory effect upon a protected minority. E.E.O.C. complaints greatly complicate dismissal proceedings, or even summative evaluations. E.E.O.C. complaints can be used by an incompetent teacher as a very effective means of harassment. The information requested pursuant to an E.E.O.C. investigation is another example, whereby extra work and expense can be reduced with effective documentation. However, responding to an E.E.O.C. complaint takes time and resources. Below are typical questions pursuant to an E.E.O.C. investigation. This information was taken from a questionnaire actually received. The only changes made were those necessary to protect identities and maintain clarity.

1. Notice: You are required to complete the enclosed Certification of Documents. It is necessary for the certification to accompany any copies of documents submitted in response to the Request for Information. Please note that this certification *must* be notarized.
2. What is your official/legal name? If different from above, please indicate name under which you do business. Explain the nature of your business.
3. Is your organization a government contractor? If so, please submit a copy of the most recent compliance review.
4. What prior conciliation agreements have been entered into or what

discrimination suits have been filed against your organization? Identify by style, suit, statute, basis, issues, and civil action number.

5. Are you a parent/subsidiary company? If so, provide the name and address of the parent/subsidiary company.

6. In addition to any of the information requested herein, submit a written position statement on each allegation of the charge, accompanied by documentary evidence, affidavits, and other written statements, where appropriate, including any additional information and explanation you deem relevant to the charge.

7. Include signed statements from (name of principal), (name of supervisor), and (name of assistant for instruction) regarding the Charging Party's allegations in the charge.

8. Submit a copy of Charging Party's complete personnel file, including evaluations and disciplinary actions.

9. Submit a copy of assistant for instruction's complete personnel file, including evaluations and disciplinary actions, if any.

10. Submit position descriptions for (all personnel involved) for the school year (_____).

11. State what requirements of the job the Charging Party failed to meet and append supportive documentation.

12. Have other teachers been disciplined during (_____) for like and similar reasons the Charging Party or for other reasons? If so, provide a copy of their personnel file, including all disciplinary actions and evaluations.

13. It is the policy or practice to (whatever the problem)? Explain in detail and if there is a written policy, provide a copy of same.

14. Submit the name, title, and personnel records of all teachers who are assigned problem children, and identify the number of such children assigned to each teacher.

15. Submit copies of the following policies and procedures:
    a. Disciplinary policy,
    b. Evaluation policy,
    c. Assessment for professional development manual, and
    d. State rules and regulations governing evaluation procedures.

A Question of Authority

Note that some very confidential information is requested regarding students and persons not involved in the complaint. Whether the E.E.O.C. has authority to force violation of a third party's right to confidentiality appears to be unsettled. Before responding to a questionnaire similar to the above, it is suggested that this concern be discussed with an attorney. As was suggested earlier, it is advisable to involve the school board attorney at an early stage when litigation appears to be likely.

Complete documentation is necessary to answer E.E.O.C. complaints. The authority of E.E.O.C. appears to be quite comprehensive; therefore, documentation takes on an even greater significance.

SOME LEGAL ASPECTS OF TERMINATION

Property Rights

The legal aspects of termination are voluminous; however, there are two basic interrelated concepts which always must be considered in possible job terminations. These are the concepts of property rights and due process. Property rights become an issue when the government (i.e., a quasi-municipal corporation legally charged to conduct a state function, such as a school system) seeks to take away an employee's job which he or she has, through tenure or contract, the legal expectancy of retaining. Article V of the Constitution of the United States states in part, that a person has the right not to be "deprived of life, liberty, or property, without due process of law . . ."

When employment becomes a property right, termination must be done only with due process. The concept of due process incorporates substantive and procedural components. Substantive due process is that aspect of the due process requirement in which the concern is whether or not the substance of charges for dismissal relate to a legitimate interest and requirement of the employer. Of course, such interest or requirements cannot usurp the protected rights of the employee. For example, a school board policy which requires all male teachers to belong to the Kiwanis Club raises questions, among other things, of the teacher's right to substantive due process. A school board would be hard pressed to show a legitimate relationship between the exercise of teaching and this policy.

Due Process

Procedural due process concerns fair play. Most states have procedural due-process requirements written into state statutes. Of course, procedural due process extended to a teacher who has a property interest must comply with the Fourteenth Amendment of the Constitution and applicable common law (judicial interpretations). Basic requirements of procedural due process encompass, at least, the following:

1. Right to receive notice of charges
2. Right to a hearing
3. Right to representation
4. Right to see or hear evidence
5. Right to call witnesses
6. Right to cross-examine witnesses
7. Right to receive a written response

The concept of due process is fluid and dynamic. Nontenured teachers do not enjoy the same due-process rights as tenured teachers because of the concept of property interest. As mentioned before, one of the most important aspects of the attorney's job is to make sure due-process rights are accorded to those considered for termination.

The Administrator's Dilemma

Many members of the general public do not understand property rights and due process. They do not consider that a dismissal, particularly for those with tenure, is, indeed, an example of the government taking away a property right. The administrator, in the effort to do his or her job correctly and legally, may hear, "Why the delay?" "Doesn't anyone in the schools have the courage to move against incompetence?" Regardless of public pressure, it is wise to move correctly because of the dynamic nature of due process. It is wise to be certain that all necessary rights are accorded to those considered for termination.

Being an Effective Witness

After all the documentation has been completed and after the first stages of due process have been initiated, the hearings ensue. Possibly, there are hearings before the school board, the local court of competent jurisdiction, and the federal district court; of course, some states have special commissions or tribunals to hear local conflicts related to dismissal proposals. Being an effective witness is critical. In fact, witnessing effectively is as critical as careful documentation.

There are four areas of concern that relate to effective witnessing: (1) fielding tough questions; (2) dress; (3) physical demeanor; and (4) organization. Each concern will be discussed briefly.

Fielding Tough Questions. The opposing attorney or advocate tends to ask questions that may lead to some unforseen trap. In this situation, there is a tendency for a witness to respond in one of the following ways:

1. To stall while trying to figure where the opponent is going with the line of questioning. Stalling may cause a witness to talk in circles, stammer, or to say, "uh . . . and uh . . ."
2. To answer in a defensive tone or display defensive body language.
3. To become visibly upset with the opposing attorney—and to make responses, such as, "I see what you are implying, and it won't work . . ."

All of the above can have a negative impact upon those who must render a decision. A look at some positive rules for fielding tough questions may be useful.

1. *Make sure the question is understood:* Time to think can be purchased by asking for a repeat or clarification, but a witness projects "stalling" if this method is overused.
2. *Answer the question calmly:* If the question is misleading, your attorney will intervene or will return to the point later.
3. *Treat the opposing attorney with respect:* Attempting to argue with the opposing attorney or to make him or her look bad does not help.
4. *Talk about the effect of actions:* The fact that a teacher left work early is not as important as stating "a written policy was violated when the teacher's class of twenty-five was left unsupervised. Other classes were also disturbed as a result of his leaving his class."

Dress. When witnessing, the most appropriate way to dress is in a conservative business manner. Visualize how the judge might dress if he were not wearing a robe. The following basic guidelines are in order for men; of course, correlative attire applies to women:

1. Dark suit (blue or gray)
2. White shirt
3. Conservative tie
4. Black socks
5. Black shoes or wing tip

Typical clothes to avoid are these:

1. Matching socks and ties
2. Colored shirts
3. Loud ties
4. Sports coats
5. Brown shoes

One's attire says many things: e.g., "This person is serious"; "This person is solid"; "This person is trendy"; "This person is a lightweight." When one is witnessing, it is important for everything to convey a sound image.

Physical Demeanor. Personal actions or body language can contribute to or detract from a person's credibility. Some suggestions are these:

1. Sit erect, but not in a stiff manner.
2. Keep arms and legs uncrossed.
3. Keep hands in a relaxed position—avoid fooling with fingernails, hair, ear, nose, or anything else.
4. Don't change posture when questions are hostile or insulting

Organization. Being organized as a witness is second only in importance to the actual information you have to contribute. Organization involves reviewing the sequence of events, and being sure that you are familiar with dates and times. For example, in an actual case that was observed, an opposing attorney almost discredited a witness because of confusion over a date; in reality, the exact date was of little importance.

It is important not to make assumptions or to speculate. Only testify about what you *know* to be a fact. The same is true about asking questions. Don't ask or encourage your attorney to ask questions, unless you are absolutely sure of the answer or have a concrete rebuttal to offer if the anticipated answer is not given. As a witness, or as one of the advisatory parties, you are there to state facts and effects from a previous investigation that has been documented. Probing questions are best left to the judge, commissioner, or board member who is conducting the hearing. Both attorneys and administrators have been "hung out to dry" because of careless probing or, as it is called, "fishing expeditions."

When getting organized, a helpful procedure is to make an organizational chart. This might resemble the one shown in Figure 7-2. It serves as a "thumbnail" sketch for quick review. Your attorney can also use this chart in reviewing your proposed testimony. Yes! Before the hearing, all witnesses for the administration

PROBLEM	DATE	EFFECT	ACTION	OTHER

Figure 7-2 A Sample Organizational Chart for Witnessing.

and the representing attorney should conduct a practice session. This is not unethical conduct, and honesty and integrity must be the absolute criteria for the practice. There is a need for the attorney to know what will be said at the hearing. This gives him or her insight about appropriate questions to ask, the sequence of witnesses, and how to conduct the case. It gives the witnesses a chance to relate information, in a pressure-free situation, that they must later relate under a degree of stress.

All this preparation for witnessing may appear extreme or time consuming; but remember earlier advice—to lose involves very undesirable consequences for students and for the school system!

SUMMARY

The goal of evaluation is usually growth and improvement. Therefore, evaluation is most productive when it is used to assist the competent. Of course, all teachers are not competent. When evaluating the incompetent, evaluation becomes summative. Obtaining improvement is a goal, but winning in efforts to remove incompetence becomes critical.

Several ways to win while using evaluation as a terminal activity involve the use of "no-risk wins." Essentially, no-risk wins involve strategies to terminate present conditions without termination of employment. There are occasions when this strategy is the best preliminary plan to follow. Activities, such as (1) making the final effort, (2) reassigning the teacher, and (3) preparing for termination are useful strategies to effect change.

On occasion, the best of efforts do not work. These occasions make documentation a necessity. The use of a microcomputer as a tool to assist with documentation is suggested. Administrators may experience mild psychological dysfunction as a result of working through a summative evaluation and subsequent termination. These problems may be addressed by recognizing the feelings involved with termination and allowing them to surface so they may be examined.

It has been determined that the incompetent population among the teaching staff seldom exceeds two percent. To spend inordinate amounts of time with this population may not be a productive use of time.

It is possible to receive charges through the E.E.O.C. while conducting a due-process hearing or litigation locally. To lose in either arena portends, at best, the continuance of incompetent performance, which again underscores the need for careful documentation.

Finally, evaluation as a terminal activity should be from a different evaluative protocol than for teachers not experiencing severe problems. This will help prevent the productive teaching staff from becoming suspicious of the evaluation procedure. Success with terminal evaluation requires the following: (1) efforts to avoid termination; (2) careful documentation; and (3) meticulous observation of due-process rights.

chapter 8

EVALUATION AS A BASIS FOR MERIT PAY

Merit pay is a term often used for any of several pay schemes which purport to pay teachers on the basis of motivation and productivity. Actually, merit pay is one of several, rather distinct efforts to differentiate between teachers and break out of the old single-salary pay scale. Others include such programs, as "pay for performance," incentive plans, and "career ladders."

Merit pay and the other differentiated pay plans make good sense from a practical viewpoint. In fact, the programs even sound like the "American way" to pay the "good" and punish the "bad." However, from a research perspective, the odds are small that a school system can create a differentiated pay plan which will fulfill the purposes of its designers. As Figure 8-1 implies, merit pay is somewhat of a puzzle and has both positive and negative factors. As with any puzzle, some combinations create unanticipated or even unworkable outcomes. Making the pieces fit together in a merit pay plan is difficult. This is symbolized by the fact that the pieces in Figure 8-1 are not compatible, even though first appearance may indicate that they can be combined to form a rectangle.

In the following pages, ways to increase the possibility of success with differential pay plans will be discussed, and a description of a successful program will be given.

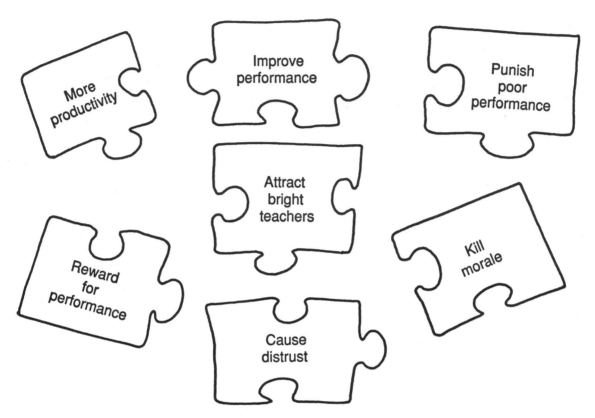

Figure 8-1 Merit Pay Puzzle.

UNDERSTANDING DIFFERENTIATED PAY

Merit Pay

The most commonly discussed form of differentiated pay is one based on merit. This is because almost all efforts at differentiation are lumped together and referred to as merit pay. Actually, merit pay is the simplest form of differentiated pay. It involves selecting the most meritorious teachers and recognizing them with higher pay. Two factors which almost always accompany merit pay are these:

1. Teachers automatically reject it.
2. Politicians love it.

This set of circumstances creates some challenges and some serendipitous circumstances. The challenge is that given just a small reason the merit pay plan will be condemned by teachers. This means that any such plan must be built on a solid basis and that fairness must be stressed to a fault. This is one activity where human error is not tolerated.

On the plus side, politicians are so enamored with the idea of merit pay that needed funds can be secured for almost anything which resembles it. This is possibly due to the ground swell in the public opinion that substantial numbers of incompetent teachers are in the schools. Anything which suggests visions of "getting the incompetent" is fully embraced in the political arena.

Cohen and Murnane* surveyed more than one hundred school systems reported as using merit pay. They identified six districts, where plans had been in effect for at least six years, for an in-depth analysis. One of their conclusions is that the operational strategies for all six merit plans implied a redefinition of merit pay. None of the districts studied made merit pay dependent upon classroom performance.

Where merit pay has been in effect for some time, it appears that an accommodation is reached which, in fact, eliminates the factors the public commonly associates with merit pay. This co-opting tends to happen to all differentiated pay plans. Of course, there is always need for midcourse corrections, but diligence and devotion to original goals are required to keep the plan from being so changed that the original purpose is lost. The question is not whether merit pay produces any benefits, but how long will it last before its redefined structure results in loss of original concept?

Problems associated with merit pay are abundant and are identified as occurring under one of the following broad categories:

1. Problems with program design
2. Problems with the evaluation system
3. Problems with teacher morale

There is one other problem with merit pay which makes it useless as a concept: i. e., *"to pay someone for being meritorious is to pay for what has already occurred."* The real goal is to help improve performance. If the resources are used to pay a few "stars," while the others wonder how they succeeded, there may not be resources to pay for a differentiated pay program which can help improve teaching. Since merit pay is contingent on past performance, and potential problems outweigh advantages, the adoption of such a program may be ill advised.

Incentive Pay

A differentiated pay scheme which includes the setting of a goal and pays all who reach this goal an extra stipend is incentive pay. This concept include "career ladders" and "pay for performance" plans.

---

* David Cohen and Richard J. Murnane, "Merits of Merit Pay," The Public Interest, No. 80, Summer 1985. Copies may be obtained from Stanford Educational Policy Institute, Stanford University.

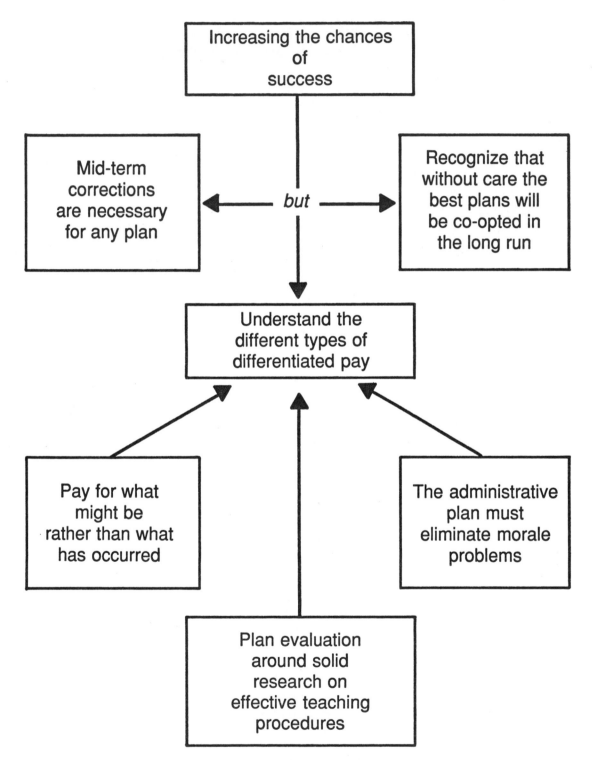

Figure 8-2 Differentiated Pay.

Pay for performance plans usually define performance in some way other than student achievement. The best pay for performance programs set research-based teaching practices as the basis for performance and pay stipends when these practices are clearly demonstrated in the act of teaching. Figure 8-2 includes suggestions for increasing the success of differentiated pay programs.

Designers of pay for performance assume that using research-based teaching practices will increase student achievement. This assumption is viewed as reasonable, because the practices were originally identified as occurring when effective teaching was taking place. (More on this particular approach, later.)

Career ladders are very popular for statewide implementation. Politicians in the statehouses tend to think that career ladders constitute some type of advanced merit pay strategy. After analyzing several career ladder plans, it is concluded that they are, at best, poor incentive plans and, at worst, simply the imposition of a parallele single-salary scale. The main difference between career ladders and the old single-salary scale is that there are a few more crevices to cross and a few more "hoops" to jump. For example, career ladders typically include such items as summer work, extended daily work, additional graduate work, and additional responsibility for some aspect of school operation or quasi-supervisory responsibility. Perhaps, a redeeming value of the career ladder is that in some states it is a politically viable way to get more money to the teacher.

THE PROBLEM WITH STUDENT ACHIEVEMENT

A well-designed pay for performance program will result in increased student achievement, but the payoff will not be a short-term one. There is a tendency for those who advocate differentiated pay to expect immediate results in student performance. For this reason, there is a push to find ways to tie pay to student achievement.

Finding a direct connection to student achievement is one of the greatest frustration points for designers of differentiated pay. A connection to achievement can be made, but there are many variables to control, and the administrative component becomes extremely difficult to manage. Finally, most efforts are unsuccessful or abandoned, because the resulting administrative quagmire distracts from other instructional and service programs.

Note that this is not a claim that merit pay or some other form of differentiated pay cannot be connected to achievement. A simple, clear-cut strategy to establish this connection will probably be developed during the present decade, owing to the proliferation of solid research about learning and the quantum strides in computer technology. At the present time, however, efforts are not simple to administer or to control because of the multitude of variables involved.

Planning the Finances

There is one financial constant with differentiated pay. It will cost more than anticipated! The increased cost occurs chiefly, because there is a tendency for a larger number of teachers to qualify than was originally planned.

To limit participation almost dooms a differentiated pay program from the start. A limit harms morale and leads to competition and hostility among teachers.

Once the standards for extra pay are set, there is a tendency for most teachers to qualify. This tendency may not be visible immediately, but it will occur during the period of a few years. In fact, this phenomenon is a direct result of one of the wonderful aspects of working with teachers. *When teachers know the standard, most will make a dedicated effort to achieve it.* It must be obvious that setting standards in an attempt to quantify excellence is a residual benefit of differentiated pay.

INITIATING DIFFERENTIATED PAY

The first step in initiating differentiated pay is to gain some understanding of the concept. The last few pages have been devoted to this effort. It was mentioned earlier that the problems with merit pay arise in one or more of three main areas. This is also true, to a lesser extent, with differentiated pay. In Figure 8-3, some of the aspects of design, evaluation, and morale are illustrated. Note that the antithesis of a problem is a possibility for its successful resolution. Note, as well, that morale is treated as a separate component. However, a serious problem with any component of the plan usually has consequences for morale.

In the figure, "large cash bonuses" are listed as a detriment to success. This may appear unusual, or even as opposed to the concept of differentiated pay; but teachers are different from most professional personnel, and money is of limited value as a motivator. In fact, there is ample research to support the concept that money is not a motivator at all, but a creator of discontent when not paid in adequate amounts; that is, money may not cause teachers to work harder, but if it is not available in reasonable amounts, its absence will create morale problems which will detract from work.

If money will not motivate, why use differentiated pay? There are several adequate responses to this question.

1. The public believes it will motivate.
2. It presents a chance to provide, at least, some teachers with professional salaries.
3. It may help to restore self-esteem to a profession which has been maligned to such an extent that some of its members have identity problems.

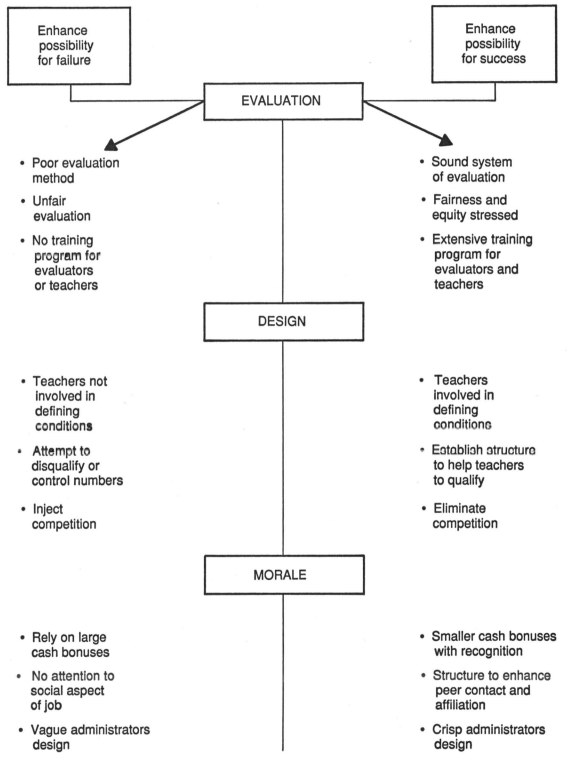

Figure 8-3 Possible Procedures in Initiating Differentiated Pay.

129

4. With a little effort, it can underscore recognition, which is a motivator.

Back to the problem of large bonuses—when the money at stake is large, (more than few hundred dollars per year, perhaps), the differentiated pay scheme causes the development of less patience for any human weakness among those involved. The stakes get too high, and the school climate changes to one of distrust, anxiety, and competition.

Small bonuses or differentials are workable. This is particularly true if relatively small school resources are spent to strengthen the recognition given to those who meet the criteria for extra pay, and if small bonuses are given in lump sums. Some examples of ways to give this recognition follow:

1. Recognition dinners or breakfasts.
2. Extra funds for classroom supplies (perhaps a few hundred dollars).
3. Special coffees with the superintendent while substitutes or volunteers cover classes.
4. Special business cards furnished by the school system.
5. Opportunities to conduct training for new teachers and others trying to qualify for extra pay.
6. Opportunities to represent the school system with visitors or as presenters at conferences.

There are literally dozens of ways to let successful teachers know that they are very significant human beings. When money is tied to recognition, the money probably gives an excuse or serves as an impetus for doing the rest. For this reason, extra money is very important, even if its reputation as a motivator is tarnished.

DIFFERENTIATED PAY—THE PROMISE

All the cautions given and assaults upon merit pay, career ladders, and pay for performance may create the impression that differentiated pay is a poor concept. However, this is not true; differentiated pay is viewed as perhaps the only viable route for relieving some of the very real dilemmas of the teaching profession.

There are almost three million teachers in the United States. Common sense indicates that members of such a large group cannot receive significantly larger salaries. This assessment is more accurate than ever before, because there is a growing tendency toward downgrading the pay for the middle-class worker, as the country adjusts from a manufacturing economy to a technological and service-oriented economy. It becomes a concern not only for the middle class, but for other segments of society as well.

The middle class, with goals toward upward mobility and a value system which supports public education as the road to a better life, has been a traditional bastion of support. With the middle class now coming under stress, it is very doubtful that the tax base required to raise the average teacher's salary by at least fifty percent can be created, or that such an increase could be maintained.

In all teacher salaries cannot be increased by more than the normal amount, which is usually between five and ten percent per year, perhaps a structure can be created that would permit some teachers to ascend to a professional pay status. There are many categories for differentiated pay—master teachers, lead teachers, research teachers, etc. Most of these programs are designed to remove that aspect of the profession which allows little or no possibilities for position growth and to make certain that the profession is not conceived of as "dead end."

The traditional route of advancement for a teacher is from teaching to school-level administration and to central-office administration. This process has been broadly assaulted for good reason, since it takes those with motivation away from teaching. In reality, with recent improvements in salary, many top teachers will choose not to consider entering the field of administration. The fact is that administration is not viewed as a desirable, upward destination by many teachers. A few reasons for this phenomenon are the following:

1. Teachers are reaching for new professional pride and resent the idea of leaving the classroom for a "promotion."
2. The salary differential between a beginning administrator and an experienced teacher is not significant, especially if extra days and time on the job are considered.
3. The job of administrator requires the use of a higher level of confrontation than ever before.
4. The news and entertainment media often depict the administrator in an undesirable manner, and the common culture within university schools of education contains an anti-administration bias.

With the traditional ways for teachers to achieve promotion having lost much appeal, and with a need to create new structures in order to allow some vertical movement in a parallel profession, the adoption of a differentiated pay plan offers promise. Even though certain forms of differentiated pay are not very promising, it is gratifying to see experimentation. At the least, this interest indicates that there are educators who are willing to take risks in seeking solutions.

A PROGRAM THAT WORKS

The pay for performance plan of the Orange County (Virginia) Schools has received attention and recognition on a nationwide basis. By design, it is a model plan. The plan has been developed as an attempt to accomplish the specific purposes of affecting student achievement by involving school staff in research-based teaching practices, which include the following:

1. Involve teachers in meaningful staff development activities
2. Involve competent teachers as teachers of other teachers
3. Provide teachers with additional opportunities to visit other teachers who are engaged in teaching
4. Provide a vehicle for additional responsibility and recognition
5. Change the school ethos to one where the quality of teaching is discussed and valued
6. Involve all teachers with the evaluative instruments in a positive way
7. Change most supervision to the positive mode
8. Involve peer evaluators
9. Make a small amount of extra pay available to motivated teachers

Evaluation Program Already Working

It has been stated that the evaluation system is one of the problems with differentiated pay. In the Orange County case, the program for teacher evaluation was well established. In fact, the evaluation system had been created with heavy involvement of teachers and administrators. Both had been members of research teams who had identified teaching practices that worked. This system was based on the latest research and the best thinking of outstanding teachers and administrators.

The Orange County plan gives us a useful rule to follow: *before considering differentiated pay, a solid teacher evaluation system should be in place.*

With an evaluation system in use which had been developed in consultation with Orange County's teachers and for which there was wide, spread teacher acceptance, half the work needed for the pay for performance plan was complete. The following tasks remained to be completed:

1. Set the desired standard for receiving performance pay
2. Decide how to collect information
3. Project cost, and secure funding
4. Set operational procedures

There were twelve professional practices in the evaluation system. Previous experience had shown that it was difficult for a teacher to demonstrate all these practices in a single year. It was also very difficult for an evaluator to observe twelve professional practices and the ten or twelve performance indicators which defined each.

Through communication with teachers, it was decided that in-depth concentration on three professional practices per year would be suitable for the teachers and observers. The twelve professional practices indentified were the following:

1. Classroom routines
2. Essential techniques of instruction
3. Provisions for individual learning
4. Lesson plans and objectives for learning
5. Evaluation of student progress
6. Critical thinking and problem solving
7. Teacher-student rapport
8. Student motivation
9. Management of student behavior
10. Student participation in learning activities
11. Reports and routine duties
12. School and community relations

For an example of a professional practice and the accompanying performance indicators, refer to Chapter 3.

There were three standards established as levels of teacher performance. These were—insufficient, competent, and proficient. "Insufficient" means that the same professional practice would be targeted for the ensuing year. "Competent" meant that the professional practice was complete. Achieving a "competent" rating did not result in incentive pay; the teacher had the option of selecting the same professional practice for another year to try for the performance pay. The rating of "proficient" paid a stipend.

An approximation of what might be required with a professional practice of ten performance indicators is listed below:

- Insufficient: Demonstrates less than four performance indicators.
- Competent: Demonstrates six or more of the performance indicators.
- Proficient: Demonstrates at least nine of the performance indicators

Collection of Information

The evaluation instrument was in place; the standards were set; and the decision making then focused on the collection of information. This involved the following decisions:

1. Who would collect the information?
2. What would be the protocol for information collection?
3. Who would evaluate the information collected?

It is difficult to separate the identification of the collectors of information from the protocol. In the Orange County plan, these two aspects of the program were designed together. Therefore, the following discussion will give background about both the collectors (peer observers) and the protocol for collecting.

It was decided that the collecting of information and evaluating this information for pay for performance was too time consuming a job for the school principal. Also, the principal was heavily involved in summative evaluations.

The decision was made to make the pay for performance program evaluations formative. It was the principal's job to make summative evaluations and subsequent recommendations. Formative and summative evaluations were kept separate.

It can be argued that a pay for performance assessment, by its very nature, is summative. Possibly, the Orange County Program "begged the issue." However, there are other operational procedures which make the pay for performance program formative. Some of these procedures involve peer observers observing only from a positive protocol.

It was decided that teachers should be trained as peer observer, and each teacher would receive a minimum of six in-depth observations per year. The peer observers would collect the information for the performance pay. Each professional practice was to be assessed at least twice. Each of the assessments was conducted by a separate peer evaluator. This increased the chance of getting an accurate assessment.

One of major issues to be resolved with the teachers was how to select peer observers. The peer observers received several status items, such as recognition as competent to assess others' performance, extra pay for making the assessments, and a limited amount of released time to attend the duties of peer observer. Consensus was finally reached through an interesting and productive approach. The peer observers were selected initially on the basis of a previous year's satisfactory evaluation, tenure, extra responsibilities assumed, and willingness to attend extensive training. A peer observer was allowed to hold the position for only three consecutive years. With thirty-five observers, this kept the position rotating and created opportunities for a larger number of teachers to serve as peer observers. It also created opportunities for a large number of teachers to rotate through the training and therefore generated broader school staff interest in the plan.

Once the decision was made to use peers, there was consensus that teachers would not critique each other, find fault, or report problems to the administrators. It was believed that criticism would soon destroy any benefits of a pay for performance program. This led to a decision to allow only positive feedback.

Then the Orange County program is discussed, a usual question arises: "How can teaching practices be improved if teachers are not told what they are doing wrong?" This question may be answered by a few observations:

1. On a scale of one to ten, criticism is the second or third worst technique for improving performance.
2. Modeling is the most effective way to improve performance.
3. Successful modeling by the learner of a carefully stated expectancy leads to adoption.
4. Having successful performance recognized and reinforced leads to its adoption.
5. Persons who are free from the fear of criticism will seek assistance in order to achieve recognition.

A significant part of the Orange County program was that peer observers were not allowed to criticize. They observed a single professional practice at a time and identified each performance indicator performed in the practice of teaching. When a performance indicator was identified (modeled), a brief sentence was written describing exactly what was observed.

During an observation, the observer would perhaps write only three or four key words about each performance indicator, which would serve as a memory prop for writing the observation after class.

If a teacher did not demonstrate one or more performance indicators, a blank space was left on the observation report. If the blank space was questioned at the postconference, the observer, following procedures, did not criticize. Moreover, the observer was trained to (1) offer to return when the performance indicator might be demonstrated, (2) discuss ways of demonstrating the performance indicator, or (3) facilitate having the observed teacher visit another classroom to observe a teacher who was particularly competent in the area of concern.

The chief point to make is that the program was designed to document a teacher doing something correctly. Its goal was to help all teachers qualify for the performance pay. The program was designed to cause change by reinforcing effective teaching practices. Another of its goals was to integrate effective teaching practices into the school ethos.

To provide a system of checks and balances for both teacher and program integrity, each teacher was assigned two peer observers. Each participant completed the following steps of the total program:

1. Made a decision whether to participate
2. Chose three professional practices
3. Was assigned two peer observers
4. Had each peer observe the three professional practices
5. Had results given to principal
6. Received principal's report verifying that documented actions satisfied the appropriate performance indicators.

The principal arranged additional peer observations if there was a discrepancy in the assessment of the two observers or if the teacher did not meet the criteria on the first round. There was concern that the actions documented be of suitable quality. At the same time, if the initial documentation did not allow qualification, additional opportunities were provided. It probably cannot be over-stated that the program's goal was to reinforce effective teaching performance by observing and documenting effective teaching.

Additional Operating Procedures

There were teacher training assistants (TTAs) involved in the program during the dirst three years of its operation. TTAs were expert teachers who volunteered to become especially proficient in one or more of the professional practices. Their job was to help teachers who requested assistance. They provided teachers with either a classroom visit or assistance prior to peer assessment. They also offered assistance to those teachers who did not fully understand performance indicators.

Participation in the pay for performance program was voluntary. The participation in the Orange County system was more than ninety-five percent. Of those who participated, more than ninety percent received pay for meeting at least two of the three performance indicators.

Those who did not participate were evaluated by the principal in a traditional manner, with an assessment of current performance and job targets set for the next year.

Budget

Figure 8-4 is an actual budget plan recently used for the pay for performance system. This budget included the funds necessary for a program that included 235 teachers.

The budget in Figure 8-4 did not include any funds for the teacher training assistants, because the pay for performance has been in effect for several years, and there are an adequate number of teachers who have earned bonuses in every professional practice and who provide help to others.

Cycle Completion

The cycle completion bonus (identified above as P.E.T.) is an aspect of the Orange County Program which was added after the program was in effect. The original plan called for teachers to complete all twelve professional practices, in yearly increments of three. Upon completion, teachers repeated the process. This procedure was perceived to be appropriate, since the teacher evaluation booklet was

```
Orange County High School:
    4 Academic deans (observers)      $ 8,000.00
    74 Professional bonuses*           13,320.00
    16 P.E.T. bonuses                   8,000.00
Total                                              $29,320.00

Prospect Heights Middle School:
    6 Teacher observers               $ 6,000.00
    48 Professional bonuses*            8,640.00
    2 P.E.T. bonuses                    1,000.00
Total                                               15,640.00

Gordon-Barbour Elementary School:
    6 Teacher observers               $ 4,800.00
    28 Professional bonuses*            5,040.00
    2 P.E.T. bonuses                    1,000.00
Total                                               10,840.00

Lightfoot Elementary School
    4 Teacher observers               $ 3,200.00
    15 Professional bonuses*            2,700.00
    2 P.E.T. bonuses                    1,000.00
Total                                                6,900.00

Orange Elementary School:
    10 Teacher observers              $ 8,000.00
    42 Professional bonuses*            7,560.00
    2 P.E.T. bonuses                    1,000.00
Total                                               16,560.00

Unionville Elementary School:
    5 Teacher observers               $ 4,000.00
    21 Professional bonuses*            3,780.00
    2 P.E.T. bonuses                    1,000.00
Total                                                8,780.00

TOTAL PAY FOR PERFORMANCE BUDGET                   $88,040.00


    * Two lump-sum payments of $90.00—one before Christmas and the other at the end
of the school year.
```

Figure 8-4 Budget Plan.

also revised on a two- or three-year schedule. Therefore, by the time a teacher completed all professional practices, it was assumed that there would be new material and a need to repeat the process. With each cycle completion, the teacher could become even more expert in this continuing program.

With the attention given to career ladders on a nationwide basis, teachers expressed interest in adopting a career-ladder-type bonus as a cycle completion stipend. Both teachers and administrators began to evaluate how larger bonuses could be incorporated into the existing program. The teachers proposed a significant bonus at the end of each four-year cycle. This concept was not received enthusiastically by the superintendent, because the bonus, once achieved, would become a part of the teacher's yearly salary for the remainder of the teacher's career. The bonus would be retained with no regard to future performance and would increase the cost of the program significantly.

A compromise was reached. A one-time cycle completion bonus was paid each time the teacher completed the cycle. A list of the most critical performance indicators was compiled. This list was named the Procedures for Effective Teaching (P.E.T.). After completing an assessment cycle (usually in four years), a teacher was given the option to work with P.E.T. for one year. Upon completing P.E.T., the teacher was paid a cycle completion bonus.

The P.E.T. was observed in a manner similar to the other professional practices, except that the performance indicators needed to be demonstrated with a degree of frequency. In other words, it was expected that the use of these critical performance indicators would become a regular part of the teaching protocol. At the end of each four-year cycle, the teacher had the option of working with P.E.T. and receiving a cycle completion bonus. In looking at the budget (Figure 8-4), notice the two P.E.T. bonuses for each elementary school. This is due to the fact that some teachers were encouraged to move forward in three years due to a need to balance the budgetary obligations.

It has been noted by many who have visited the school system and observed the program in action that the money allotted was meager. This is true! However, if five times the resources were added, the program would probably be destroyed. Significant additional resources would possibly create suspicion, pressure, and jealousy. At the present time, there is an intent to increase the finances of the program, but in increments.

Teacher Acceptance

Clarence Edwards, a teacher at Orange County High School, served as the leader for teacher input during the program's inception. He shared much thought and provided clear insight about the needs of the teachers and how to mesh these needs with those of policy makers. The program was first piloted in a single school—Orange County High School—and then adopted on a county-wide basis. One year after its system-wide adoption, Mr. Edwards conducted a teacher survey. Some of his initial results are shown in Figure 8-5.

A summary listing of operational procedures of the Orange County Pay For Performance Program is given below:

1. The pay for performance Program was based upon an existing evaluation system and was a voluntary extension of that system.
2. Teachers were heavily involved in designing both the evaluation system and the pay for performance program.
3. Except for first-year teachers, the teachers selected the performance indicators. (all indicators had to be eventually accomplished for qualification of a cycle completion bonus.)
4. Participation was voluntary.

% OF RESPONDENTS			
YES	?	No	
92	6	1	The teacher should be able to control when the observer will be in the classroom.
88	8	1	Teachers should be able to control which practice is to be observed.
81	15	3	Proficient teachers should be used to assist new teachers.
81	6	9	Participation in the incentive pay program should be voluntary.
72	18	8	The observation reports of my classroom presentations do fairly reflect what I do.
71	17	10	My observation reports make me feel better about the job I am doing.
69	20	8	Although the observer only reported my strengths in the classroom, my teaching performance has improved this year.
67	23	5	I expect that over a period of time my classroom observations reports will accurately reflect my teaching performance.
63	25	9	The observation reports prepared by my teacher-observers give the principal a better picture of what I do in my classroom than in the past.
62	15	16	The teacher should be given several observations to demonstrate proficiency in a professional practice.
48	8	41	I did some things differently this year to become proficient in at least one of my targeted practices

Figure 8-5 Results Taken from Pay for Performance Program Survey.

5. A teacher input committee was established, whose sole purpose was to identify problems with the program and propose solutions.

6. The program was funded with the anticipation that each teacher would receive pay for performance.

7. The goal was to assist each teacher to meet the standard.

8. Peer observers did the assessments.

9. Building administrators were responsible for providing administrative support, such as establishing schedules, keeping records, helping arrange for assistance and assessments.

10. For smooth operation of the program, administrative accountability was kept at the building level.

11. All peer observers were trained extensively.

12. All administrators received the same training as peer observers.

SUMMARY

The title of this chapter, *Evaluation As A Basis For Merit Pay*, is somewhat of a misnomer. Early in the chapter, it was revealed that merit pay is perhaps one of the least desirable forms of differentiated pay. Possibly, the most serious problem with merit pay is that payment of resources is for past performance rather than as a gauge for present performance.

A performance-based pay system is suggested as perhaps the most viable type of a differentiated pay program. There is a tendency to define performance in noncontroversial ways, such as performance criteria used in career ladders. However, pay for performance is most productive when performance is tied to the existing evaluation system. This is particularly true when the evaluating system reflects research-based effective teaching practices.

Those designing new differentiated pay programs need to recognize that the purposes of the program should be identified first. This procedure has two effects:

1. The original design of the program tends to be more productive and easier to administer if designers reference its purposes as a focal point for creativity.

2. Subsequent revisions can be made, with original purposes as a reference point.

Proposed changes should be considered only if they are consistent with the original understanding of purpose. This will help to keep the integrity of the program. Without diligence, a differentiated pay program will deteriorate and become meaningless. Little will be required of participants, and the effect of producing change in the teaching process will become negligible.

The following is a summary checklist for developing differentiated pay systems:

_____ 1. A sound teacher evaluation system is in place and working.

_____ 2. Purposes to be accomplished have been identified.

_____ 3. A plan is devised for ensuring teacher involvement and ownership.

_____ 4. Research on differentiated pay has been thoroughly reviewed.

_____ 5. Sufficient funds can be allocated to prevent having a "cut-off" in the number who qualify.

_____ 6. A training plan for evaluators is in place.

_____ 7. Purposes of differentiated pay have been examined for consistency with central focus or system-wide goals.

_____ 8. The school board has been included in planning.

_____ 9. There is a plan to pilot the program for at least one year prior to its adoption.

_____ 10. Administrative requirements have been weighed, and tentative task assignments have been set.

_____ 11. Participation is voluntary.

_____ 12. There is a plan to inform the staff, school board, and community where program if finally devised.

There are other considerations for the adoption of differentitated pay plans, but omission of any of the above steps could create a source of difficulty.

The Orange County, Virginia, system of pay for performance was described in some detail. This program is an example of a system which was tied to an existing evaluation system. The program's chief purpose has been to encourage teachers to work extensively to meet the requirements of an evaluation system that is based on effective teaching practices.

Finally, many political and educational reasons can be cited for the consideration of differentiated pay, but there are none as dynamic as the possibility of changing teaching practice. Research now available offers guidelines for how schools can and should operate differentiated pay. The primary value of differentiated pay is to help initiate change.

chapter 9

SUMMATIVE EVALUATIONS

In Chapter 7, some aspects of summative evaluations were discussed. However, the primary focus was on working with the marginal or incompetent teachers. The basic questions to be considered in this chapter are the following: "How can those who need assistance be recognized?"; and, "What kind of summative evaluation is appropriate for all teachers?" Indeed, those in need of substantial summative help may exceed fifteen percent; but, after the best efforts, only two or three percent of these teachers will remain in the marginal category.

In the following pages, several of the primary aspects of summative evaluation will be discussed. Among these will be the purposes of summative evaluation, frequency, the construction of a summative instrument, and observation time. These and other topics should help make summative evaluation productive.

It is noteworthy that the primary thrust of this book is focused on formative assessment. This is as it should be, because the vast majority of teachers are already competent. However, it is necessary to have a means of identifying those in need of substantial assistance and have a set procedure for working with them. This procedure, of course, defines the use of the summative evaluation system.

IDENTIFYING THOSE WHO NEED SUMMATIVE EVALUATION

Summative evaluation is for accountability and status decisions. Under most circumstances, only a small percent of the faculty need to be evaluated summatively. How can these teachers be identified? First, a professional and political reality must be recognized. Even though only about fifteen percent of the teaching personnel need substantial summative assistance, all teachers must be evaluated periodically.

The accountability aspect of summative evaluation has two purposes:

1. To ensure that all teachers meet minimum standards of competency.
2. To provide assistance for those not meeting minimum standards or those who are borderline.

It can be seen, then, that two categories of teachers are evaluated summatively—those on the regular cycle, and those who are identified as needing special attention. Discussion follows on *frequency of summative evaluation, method of evaluation,* and *methods of "ongoing" summative sampling.*

Frequency of Summative Evaluations

Often the principal's time is utilized poorly by the requirement to over-evaluate the teachers. It is not unusual to find a principal working under a policy in which he or she is required to make yearly summative evaluations for each teacher.

If the school has more than twelve or fourteen teachers, the principal has a problem with evaluations. This problem usually comes to the forefront in April or May, when the principal realizes he or she is behind. The result is a race to complete the job. This has several effects—conferences are shortened to ten or fifteen minutes, the comprehensiveness of the summative evaluation is reduced, and the entire process may become superficial.

One reason for this yearly requirement is the popular notion that this procedure will cause the principal to focus on instruction. This notion is perpetrated by popular and professional literature and by teacher groups who sometimes complain that the principal doesn't know what's "going on," because he or she does not evaluate each teacher frequently.

If appropriate methods of summative sampling are used, formal summative evaluations can be done less frequently. Of course, this assumes that formative procedures, similar to those discussed previously, are in place.

A preferred schedule of frequency is for each teacher to be evaluated summatively in a formal manner on a two- or three-year cycle. Another approach is to conduct summative evaluations for each new teacher and for each teacher during the year prior to tenure. Summative evaluations for all other teachers can be conducted on a three-year cycle.

A formal summative evaluation is one that includes a preconference, an evaluation of every area defined in the summative instrument, and a postconference. As stated in Chapter 6, a follow-up plan is essential. It is usually formed on the basis of performance targets, with deadlines for their completion.

Summative Sampling

Summative sampling has, possibly, both an accountability and a status-determining function. It involves five components: (1) walking-around supervision; (2) short visits; (3) community, parent, and student input; (4) statistical review; and (5) information from teachers. All these components serve to tell the principal where extra time should be spent, who is doing a fine job, and who needs help. Of course, this sampling provides the principal with a broader view: i.e., insight into the organizational status of the school. Each of the five components will be discussed below.

Walking-around Supervision. The process of walking around the school as a means of informal summative assessment must have originated shortly after the "Old Deluder Laws." This type of supervision has recently found favor among those who write for business publications. As a result, the technique has been ascribed validity as a management technique and has regained respect in the education community.

An experienced observer can gather a vast amount of information from just walking through a school building when school is in session. For example, the walker can observe the teachers who are supervising in the classroom and the hall simultaneously during class change, those who actively teach until the end of the allocated time, those with few class-control problems, teachers with students motivated to engage in the class activities, and much more.

Long-term conclusions cannot be made from this type of supervision, unless patterns emerge from several encounters. The value of walking-around supervision is that it gives the principal greater flexibility over how to spend his or her time conducting summative evaluation. For example, if the principal tentatively concludes that there may be a class management problem in Room 15, he or she can plan additional summative activities to analyze the problem.

This example highlights the need for a special provision requirement of the summative schedule. It is recommended that the following policy statement be issued: "In addition to regularly scheduled summative assessments, the principal may evaluate summatively in a formal or informal manner, as he or she determines the need."

The schedule for walking-around supervision is important. The most productive times for the principal to be in the halls of a building is immediately before and after the first bell in the morning, and immediately before the dismissal bell in the afternoon. Other visits should be randomly scheduled with, perhaps, some extra attention given to the lunch period.

Positive actions, such as walking around or making short visits (which will be discussed next), enhance summative sampling and are usually favored by the teachers and students. In fact, an example comes to mind, which involves a discussion with a teacher who had taught in the same building for twenty-three years. The teacher noted that the principal was always in the halls before school started and that, for the few times that the principal did not appear in halls, the day just didn't seem to get off to a good start.

The fact was that this principal arrived at least one hour and fifteen minutes before the teachers. He spent time on paper work before anyone arrived. As the teachers and students arrived, he had a positive comment for all. He would not answer the phone or schedule conferences for the fifteen minutes before or after the first bell.

Short Visits. An excellent view of what is happening, relative to the teaching within a school, can be generated through short visits by the principal. Such visits usually last less than half of an instructional period. If the principal develops a regular program for short visits, the teachers and students will soon become accustomed to seeing the principal, and his or her presence will not be disruptive.

The principal should plan to make short visits to all teachers who are being given a full summative evaluation. The principal should spend at least one full period with the teacher who is being evaluated, but the preliminary and follow-up visits may be less than a class period.

Short visits are valuable tools for summative sampling: that is, they can be used by the principal to get a fairly accurate impression of the quality of teaching. During a short visit, the principal observes using the summative instrument. It is important to always follow up a short visit with a brief conference with the teacher. If a problem is noted, the principal can discuss this with the teacher and plan for an additional evaluation.

Student and Parent Input. The principal should establish several points of contact with the students and parents. Figure 9-1 includes several sources of input used by successful principals.

PARENTS	STUDENTS
(1) P. T. A. officers (2) Booster club members (3) Civic club members (4) Local gathering place (5) Merchants (6) Unsolicited calls	(1) Student council (monthly) (2) Lunches with students (3) Summer retreats with school leadership (4) Weekly round table (5) Individual volunteers (6) Talking with students at extra-curricular activities

Figure 9-1 Sources of Parent and Student Input Related to the Quality of Teaching.

Receiving student and parent input is invaluable. Of course, it is sometimes unreliable, but an experienced administrator will realize that input is perception and not necessarily fact. For the educator, it is worthwhile to remember that perception is caused by something; and, even though perception may not be factual, action is often needed to change it.

Student and parent input can be received without being unprofessional or violating the good faith of teachers. The principal can receive the information in a noncommital manner. He or she can make the parent or student feel significant and important, and without cost to others. The purpose is for the principal to gather information which may indicate a need for summative evaluation without spending time and effort in an inefficient "shotgun" approach.

Student and parent input must be treated with caution. There is potential for creating a morale problem with teachers. They must know that parent and student input will be checked thoroughly, and that teachers will always have an opportunity to respond to negative information.

Statistical Review. Often, a statistical review will reveal possible problems which need a further investigation. Some of the statistics which should be reviewed are the following:

1. Grade distribution for each teacher
2. A class absence profile—whose classes are being cut and how often
3. Disciplinary referrals
4. Test scores (standardized and criterion-referenced)

Information from Teachers. Teachers usually will not report on each other in an overt manner. However, in final analysis, most teachers do not want incompetent performance in their school. A competent teacher will usually give some indication if he or she is aware of another teacher's incompetent performance. The message is apt to be so subtle that it will be missed unless the principal is very perceptive. An example of this kind of subtle report is given in the following conversation:

> ***Superintendent: "I guess you are enjoying the new supplemental books."***
> ***Teacher: "I sure am, but my children seem so distracted lately that I am having to make extra effort to keep them on-task."***
> ***Superintendent: "I wonder what's causing the problem."***
> ***Teacher: "This has been going on for almost a week."***

Note that the teacher did not offer to speculate on the cause of the problem—but informed the superintendent of its duration. This was the answer! The superintendent knew that a new teacher had been employed next door one week earlier. Mrs. Smith was actually saying, "You should get someone to do something about the teacher next door."

The Summative Schedule

Identifying those who are to receive summative evaluation is usually based on a schedule, such as a two- or three-year cycle. Sometimes, the schedule used provides summative evaluation for all new teachers and those about to receive tenure. A cyclic approach is used for all others. As mentioned previously, the second way to identify those who will be evaluated summatively is to utilize summative sampling. Of course, a combination of an orderly cycle that is supplemented with a few extra evaluations based upon summative sampling is preferable.

DESIGNING THE SUMMATIVE INSTRUMENT

Two points made earlier and which are critical for the summative instrument, are the following:

1. Evaluate that which is important to the school system.
2. A summative instrument can usually be derived from some of the essential teaching characteristics identified in the formative instrument.

There are several possible designs for summative evaluation, and each will probably complement a productive evaluation. Some preliminary recommendations for making summative evaluation productive are as follows:

1. Avoid checklists. They have potential for contributing to problems.
2. Use narrative descriptions which include "effect," whenever possible.
3. Avoid judgmental statements. Stay with that which was actually observed.
4. Be positive, even for setting targets or goals.
5. Prepare a time-on-task profile.

A competent principal will spend time analyzing the measures above. If anything appears to be unusual, a preliminary short visit should be scheduled. Often, research with the statistical indicators will reveal a few teachers who stand out with questionable statistics on at least two of the four items. This certainly is an indicator of possible need for summative evaluation.

All the summative sampling techniques provide a quick look at some aspect of current performance. They are valuable tools for helping the administrator decide where to focus energy and when formal summative evaluations need to be applied. Figure 9-2 gives a "thumbnail sketch" of summative sampling.

In constructing a summative instrument, purpose must be remembered. A summative instrument is best suited to attend to the purposes of ensuring minimum standards and setting a formal procedure for required improvement. The summative instrument helps to answer questions about retention, tenure, or improvement required to retain present status.

Figure 9-3 is a sample summative instrument. It is intended to demonstrate how a summative instrument might be constructed. It could be used as a guide, but its actual use is not recommended, as the competencies and performance areas should be decided by those at the local level.

From examining Figure 9-3, it should be obvious that many of the areas listed as "areas observed" are vague and unclear. This highlights two needs in the use of a summative sheet; (1) a written document to explain what each area means; and (2) evaluator training.

In the example given, minimum acceptable standards are the goal. It is likely that a performance target or two will be needed for each teacher observed. The performance targets can be collaboratively set. One or two performance targets are

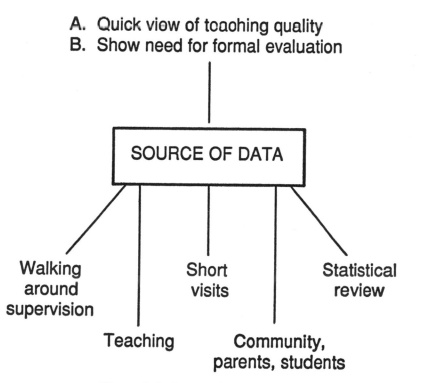

PURPOSE

A. Quick view of teaching quality
B. Show need for formal evaluation

SOURCE OF DATA

Walking around supervision

Teaching

Short visits

Community, parents, students

Statistical review

Figure 9-2 Summative Sampling.

SUMMATIVE INSTRUMENT

COMPETENCIES:	NARRATIVE

1. LESSON PLANS
    AREAS OBSERVED
       A. Objectives planned
       B. Plan relates to objectives
       C. Pre-assessment planned
       D. Formative sampling planned
       E. Plan for reteaching
       F. Enrichment strategies
       G. Summary plan
       H. Outcome measurement
	1.

2. CLASSROOM MANAGEMENT
    AREAS OBSERVED
       A. Time utilized
       B. Transitions
       C. Movement
       D. Tools and enhancements
       E. Non-verbal
       F. Discipline with dignity
	2.

3. MOTIVATION OF STUDENTS
    AREAS OBSERVED
       A. Learners told objectives
       B. Participation
       C. Questioning techniques
       D. Guided practice
       E. Reinforcement
       F. Opportunities for all to succeed
	3.

4. CONTENT PROFICIENCY
    AREAS OBSERVED
       A. Appropriateness
       B. Prescribed state and local standards
       C. Up-to-date
       D. Expertise
	4.

5. STUDENT RELATIONSHIP
    AREAS OBSERVED
       A. Corrected with dignity
       B. Know standards
       C. Assume responsibility for school as a whole
       D. Provision for student talk
       E. Positive self-image
       F. Activities varied
	5.

Figure 9-3 Sample Summative Instrument. *continued*

COMPETENCIES:	NARRATIVE

6. SCHOOL SUPPORT
    AREAS OBSERVED
      A. Extracurricular
      B. Extra duties
      C. Peer relationship
      D. Attend morale of group
      E. Parent relationships
      F. Community role
      G. Enthusiasm
	6.

7. POLICY
    AREAS OBSERVED
      A. School regulations
      B. School board policy
      C. Attendance
      D. Punctuality
      E. Records
      F. Ethical
	7.

Figure 9-3 Sample Summative Instrument. (*cont.*)

adequate. If there is a glaring deficiency, then the principal may insist that the teacher concentrate on at least one of the targets in the deficient area. As with all conferencing, a follow-up is critical for success.

Standards for Performance

It is useful to use collaboration, not only for structuring the summative instrument but also for setting the standards or minimum expectancies. Involvement is the most vital ingredient for success in evaluation. In setting the standards, remember that a summative instrument is designed to ensure minimum competency. If this author were setting the minimum expectancy for the summative instrument in Figure 9-3, he would set the standards listed in Figure 9-4.

The positive features of this type of summative evaluation are as follows:

1. With positive documentation of a majority of the performance areas, minimum competency is a high probability.
2. Choice is provided since demonstrating competence in all areas is not required.
3. A teacher can qualify in the required areas, but still have a problem

The Following Minimum Requirements Might Be Set* for the sample summative instrument (Figure 9-3):

(1) Lesson plans:
    At least five of the eight areas documented
(2) Classroom management:
    At least four areas, including A and K
(3) Motivation of students:
    At least four areas, including A and G
(4) Content:
    At least three areas, including C
(5) Student relationship:
    At least four areas, including A and D
(6) School support:
    At least four areas
(7) Policy:
    At least three areas

*Documentation is required by written narrative in accordance with the school system's written explanation of performance areas.
    A severe problem with any area may postpone minimum competence until corrective action is taken.

Figure 9-4 Minimum Requirement for Summative Evaluation.

severe enough in a single area to prevent competence. This could postpone competence.

Some problems with this type of summative evaluation are the following:

1. More effort is required than with checklists.
2. In-service training is required so that both teachers and evaluator know what each area entails.
3. Multiple observers would increase validity.

What Next?

Summative evaluation is usually sufficient for most teachers. It is an excellent way to ensure minimum acceptable quality. However, if problems persist after reasonable efforts and a summative evaluation, the next step is some type of plan of assistance. Refer to Chapter 7 for guidance in creating "final step" strategies.

About Pedagogy

To a large extent, pedagogy means teaching lots of people to do many of the things that a few people do naturally. Why is this statement shocking or disagreeable to many educators? The same is true in art, athletics, public speaking, selling, etc. There are those who are naturals, and one of the challenges of research is to discover what the naturals do that works. There is one additional thing that all educators know—all teachers can be taught how to perform better, exclusive of level of talent. How can we be sure that performance is improving, or that improved performance is adequate? We find the answer through evaluation—both formative and summative.

WHO EVALUATES SUMMATIVELY?

Summative evaluation is designed for ensuring that the minimum acceptable standards, are met. Those who evaluate summatively must make decisions which determine status, and these decisions are based upon the requirements to meet minimum standards. Most often, the principal is the person who conducts summative evaluation. The principal is the first-line administrator who must recommend tenure, retention, promotion, and who must make other status decisions. For these reasons, he or she should be the primary evaluator. It is proposed that, in most cases, the principal be clearly identified as the summative evaluator. As such, he or she usually cannot offer much formative assessment assistance. The principal can, however, serve as a facilitator of formative activities.

If the school focus is one which promotes growth, the principal will strive to keep summative work to a manageable level and ensure support for a comprehensive growth program. What about the use of central office supervisors and assistant principals as summative evaluators? This is desirable, particularly if these persons are not used formatively, or if a clear distinction in roles can be made.

It is perceived that there is very little possibility for successfully splitting roles and having a supervisor wear both a summative and a formative hat. For this reason, "teaching content" was not mentioned as a prominent part of formative assessment. In fact, it is listed as an area for summative evaluation. If the principal is in a serious summative situation, there is need for external verification. This usually thrusts the supervisor into a summative posture. In most school systems, the supervisor serves as content specialist, or is the key person who arranges for outside expertise.

Let us again pose the question: Should others do summative evaluation? In most schools, assistance with the summative sampling techniques can be accomplished by assistants to principals or supervisors, but the principal should conduct the formal summative evaluation.

In the larger secondary schools, the principal is often required to evaluate summatively more than twenty teachers each year. This number is only possible if a scheme is devised to manage evaluations effectively. Control is important, because the principal can do little work of quality if the only emphasis is on meeting number requirements. Some management suggestions follow:

1. Don't attempt to evaluate each teacher with a formal summative evaluation each year.
2. Use summative sampling techniques to target needs.
3. Be certain to make a short visit to all teachers who are not on the summative schedule.
4. Schedule evaluations throughout the school year. (Twenty visits in 180 days are manageable. Twenty visits during the last two months of school can be a "back breaker"!)
5. Be certain that all teachers understand the summative program, the schedule, and the purpose.
6. Only take on one or two serious problems at a time.

Item 5 is particularly important, because most professionals aren't yet fully aware of the differences between summative and formative evaluation, and because there are many teachers who operate under traditional assumptions. These teachers may feel that someone is "letting them down" unless they get the full treatment each year. (Funny thing about human beings—we even miss a toothache!)

VALUING

Much has been mentioned or implied about demonstrating that each person is a valuable human being. This concept is particularly true for teacher evaluation. There are some administrators who believe that, by its very nature, summative evaluations must be harsh and threatening: "Teachers meet these minimum standards, or else." This could not be further from the truth; positive human relations are even helpful in termination activities.

The concept of valuing others comes from the notion that all human beings are of worth. Most, at least, are minimally competent. Some are not competent and cannot be helped. Occasionally, those who cannot be helped can be guided in a different direction. Of course, there are times when winning (Chapter 7) takes on importance. In these instances, winning becomes the highest priority. However, the goal can be achieved through preparation and competence. Ethics and human caring can remain.

Often, administrators who evaluate teachers as failures in the classroom cannot envision these teachers as being successful in other fields. This is not true! Most experienced administrators have seen some teaching failures make excellent businesspersons, doctors, engineers, ministers, and salespersons. No doubt, each of these professions requires working with people, but teaching requires skills that are unique to the profession.

How is valuing accomplished in a hostile or personally threatening situation? The following may be helpful:

1. Make a personal connection.
2. Be patient with rationalization.
3. Resent the problem, not the person.
4. Be concerned.

Making the personal connection means to recognize the humanity of the other person through genuine personal interest. Be alert; know what has meaning to the other person; and be able to discuss these matters briefly, even if the conversation must eventually turn to improvement that must be forthcoming.

When performance is a problem, rationalization is likely to occur. Be patient. Accept the rationalization as the other person's perception, but get back to the point of what must happen. If the person is valued, the problem of concern can be hated. Separate the two. When administrator realizes that he feels hostile toward the problem or its effect rather than about the teacher, the problem is often easier to remediate. When the teacher is valued, the possibility of litigation is reduced, even though termination must be the end result.

Being concerned with helping teachers to perform satisfactorily is a characteristic sensed early by those with whom the administrator must work. Genuine concern helps to take some of the fear and anxiety from the other person when improvement is attempted. Of course, this view is not to be equated with assuming ownership or responsibility for the other person's problem.

There are those who have high expectancies, insist on performance, and terminate incompetents. Some are sued almost every time they take a job action, and others are never sued. Is the difference valuing or documenting? Perhaps, some of both.

SUMMARY

Summative evaluating is a procedure with limited purposes and specific utility. Its purposes are to ensure minimum quality and to serve as the basis for assisting those who do not meet the minimum standard. The utility of the summative evaluation is to underscore that which is significant to the school system relative to the teaching function. It also forms the basis for making status decisions about individual teachers.

The goal of summative evaluation is to get minimum competence documented, and then to proceed to formative assessment. It is in the formative mode that the reach toward excellence is accomplished.

Most summative evaluations will run smoothly, because most teachers are at least minimally competent. In teaching minimally, competent is being able to demonstrate performance in areas identified as essential for maintaining current status. Some might call this as being documented as, at least, average. Those who do not meet the summative criteria set job targets and follow-up evaluations with the principal. For these teachers, the goal is to get out of the summative mode and into nonsummative growth programs.

For a teacher who has a serious problem in one or more teaching areas, or who is not documented in the required number of performance areas within a reasonable time, a program of assistance is created. It should be designed to provide the ultimate in assistance and may require extra resources.

Consult Chapter 7 for summative evaluation situations that may result in serious consequences—i.e., possible termination of the employment relationship. Use Chapter 7 as a companion to Chapter 9. Review Chapter 6 when confrontation becomes a possibility. These three chapters should help an administrator with some of the most difficult aspects of evaluation.

In summative evaluation, the principal should consider allocation of time. Doing so involves organization and reasonable expectancies for evaluation. Summative sampling is recommended as a way for the principal to determine who may be in need of special assistance.

Finally, valuing reduces problems in every aspect of human endeavor. Several aspects of valuing are discussed. The concept is little more than according human dignity to those who cannot perform as well as to those who can.

chapter 10

PUTTING IT ALL TOGETHER

One of the prerequisites for success in constructing, revising, or even using an evaluation system is to have a basic understanding of the concept. The initial reaction to this might be skepticism, because everyone has evaluated someone or something. However, with teacher evaluation, there are some basics which should receive special attention.

WHAT'S THE GOAL (PURPOSE)?

Teacher evaluations are used in an effort to accomplish two goals:

1. To ensure accountability (competency)
2. To promote professional growth or change

One of the primary problems of evaluation occurs when both these goals are combined into a single instrument, and when evaluation of both goals is accomplished by the same person. In most circumstances, this turns the evaluation process into little more than a procedure to harass teachers. This leads to a reemphasis of two suggestions for evaluation:

1. Separate the procedure for accountability and growth.
2. Evaluate or assess each with different personnel.

Evaluation has been cited as a vehicle for change. This is due to the fact that all components of change can be given appropriate emphasis when they are connected as shown in Figure 10-1.

WHAT TO EVALUATE

Research on school effectiveness provides much of the material for devising an evaluation system. A wealth of information is also available from successful teachers. The procedure for deciding what to evaluate includes the following:

1. Form primary research Units: The task for these units is to research effective teaching practices and devise between eight and twelve professional practices for teaching competence.
2. Form secondary research units: The tasks for each unit is to accomplish the following:
   A. Write a narrative description of one or more professional practices.
   B. Devise several performance indicators from the information contained in the narrative. (See Chapter 2 for an example.)
3. From the information generated in devising the professional practices and performance indicators, devise a summative instrument. Add the following features:
   A. Expectancies for working with others
   B. Expectancies for professional responsibilities
   C. Expectancies related to policy

   A, B, and C do not relate in a direct way to effective teaching practices, but are important for overall effectiveness of the school and morale of others.

There has been much discussion about professional practices and performance indicators. A professional practice is a broad area of teaching performance. There are dozens of professional practices which can be identified as significant aspects of teaching. These practices can be identified in somewhat of a hierarchical order, and school systems can identify a dozen or less of the most critical aspects of teaching by the addition of thoughtful performance indicators. Through these means, a large part of what it takes to be successful in the classroom can be identified.

A performance indicator is a description of a factor or a facet of a professional practice. The kind of performance indicator used in teacher evaluation is known as a *leading* indicator: that is, a factor with predictive value. For example, it is known

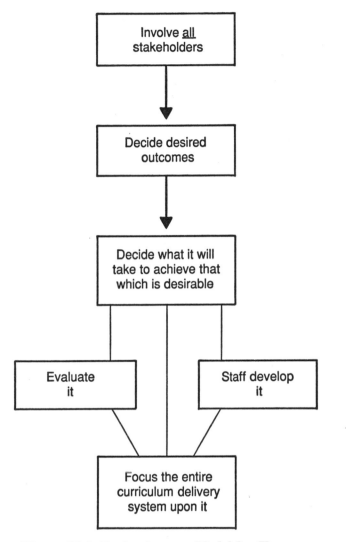

Figure 10-1 Evaluation as a Model for Change.

that learning is enhanced by a purposeful sequence of review. Therefore, if the professional practice is "lesson plans," then one of the performance indicators may be "A sequence of review is included."

If review is incorporated, it can be predicted that learning will increase. It can be seen that the professional practices are descriptive of a generally recognized teaching practice, whereas the performance indicators are descriptions of specific components of that practice.

Figure 10-2 shows a structural example of how an evaluation system may be designed. (Check the Appendix for an example of professional practices and performance indicators.)

Using Professional Practices and Performance Indicators

PROFESSIONAL PRACTICE 1:

   1.1 Performance Indicators
   1.2 _____
   1.3 _____

PROFESSIONAL PRACTICE 2:

   2.1 Performance Indicators
   2.2 _____
   2.3 _____

Figure 10-2 Using Professional Practices and Performance Indicators.

THE HUMAN ELEMENT

Much of the philosophy underlying the procedures advocated in this book embodies the belief that teachers seek to meet basic human needs as they practice their profession. In fact, positive motivation, such as ego, recognition, achievement, and the need for autonomy, is derived from attempts to meet the human needs. This leads to the basic premise that teachers will seek to achieve under the following conditions:

1. If the requirements for achievement are clearly stated
2. If others in the immediate unit value achievement
3. If recognition for achievement is provided
4. If they have confidence and ownership in the evaluation process
5. If they sense that their contributions not only are valued but also are sought.

Making teacher evaluation work is then contingent upon how we treat human beings and articulate expectancies. Specific actions recommended are the following:

1. Abandon the "good news / bad news" approach to evaluation.
2. Abandon checklist evaluations.
3. Stress involvement and ownership.

4. Adopt a positive protocol for evaluation.

5. Involve all "stakeholders."

TEACHING TEACHERS

If evaluation is used for causing growth and ensuring accountability, its by-product has to be the teaching of teachers. This is true, because the only viable way to cause change (which is a must for growth and an asset for accountability) is to have teachers learn new professional behaviors.

Evaluation should be the basis for eighty or ninety percent of the in-service training conducted in a school system. If this is not the case, the in-service activities or the evaluation system should be revamped, because something is out of "sync."

Staff Development

Staff development is the term most often used for the total program to teach teachers. There is a symbiotic relationship between evaluation and staff development. An outstanding evaluation system leads to the need for staff development, and an outstanding staff development program supports evaluation. An effective staff development system incorporates most of the folloiwng components:

1. Teacher choice in selecting activities
2. In-service directed to specific performance objectives (central focus)
3. Involvement of teachers in planning
4. Released time or pay for in-service activities
5. Incorporating opportunities for collegiality.
6. Teachers taught through modeling
7. Teachers demonstrate and observe a positive outcome.

Modeling

All of the concepts listed above are discussed in Chapter 5. Therefore, each will not be discussed again, with the exception of the concept of modeling. This concept is so important in the teaching of teachers that the earlier discussion should be expanded slightly.

Those who teach in colleges and universities have been slow to incorporate research-based teaching practices into their own personal repertoire of teaching skills. This is a problem for school systems who must rely on college personnel for preparation of teachers and in-service courses. "Tell about / read about" courses will not produce change in the learner. In this situation, the teacher simply learns about the skill or practice, but does not adopt it as a teaching practice. How can this be changed? The following are some suggestions:

1. Insist that the staff development instructors model the skills being taught.
2. Make sure that the learners also have a structured chance to model the skill being learned, such as with peer teams or learning groups.
3. To the extent possible, let competent teachers teach effective teaching practices. In fact, teachers should be utilized in all types of staff development. Teachers learn, and the teacher who teaches gains personal stature.

THE CENTRAL FOCUS

Earlier mention was made of the curriculum delivery system, which includes the evaluation system, the staff development program, the personnel department, the instructional program, and the budget office. Many times all these components of a school system are operated as independent entities, with each having separate goals, but with all being somewhat loosely connected.

A change in the traiditonal way of operating the curriculum delivery system is suggested. The curriculum delivery system and all other components of the school operation should be closely connected to support the central focus of a school system. What is the central focus? It is whatever the local school system chooses as a mission statement or set of statements. It incorporates the goals of education and embodies the belief system about the desired results of schooling.

Once the central focus is set, all components can be directed toward the outcomes necessary to achieve the focus. This gives evaluation and staff development a special significance, as each leads toward the accomplishment of requisite attitudes, philosophies, and skills necessary for accomplishing the outcomes derived from the central focus. This brings attention to the role of effective evaluation.

Evaluation is fully effective only if it relates to that which is chosen as important outcomes for students.

The local emphasis in decision making about the central focus can be noted. Of course, state and national mandates will have some impact. This impact is perceived as minimal, because creative administrators will find ways to keep the decision making close to those who are served and their direct representatives—the local school board.

The following discussion will include four areas that either impact upon how the central focus is managed or can serve as effective tools of the central focus. These areas include (1) the reform movement, (2) teacher empowerment, (3) peer evaluation, and (4) pay for performance.

The Reform Movement

The reform movement may ultimately affect teacher evaluation. This will occur only if evaluation is not understood by those who pass legislation. Of course, if the earlier chapters have been read, this statement needs no further explanation.

Quite a number of changes occurred as a result of the reform movement of the mid eighties. These changes tended to further centralize state control of public education. During the reform movement, there was an effort to move the authority of local school boards in two directions—to the state and to the teacher. As with all other components of the curriculum delivery system, the evaluation of teachers may be affected. To fully understand some of the reasons for the diverse solutions set forth in the reform movement, one needs to look at the groups involved. Who are the reformers? The answer to this question, phrased in a form of parody that bears some semblance of truth, is given below.

Politicians. This group is composed of many who are expert in education by virtue of their previous school attendance. Politicians have much in common with sports fans who are expert by virtue of their having played little league or sandlot ball. There is one striking difference, however. Even though the fans give plenty of advice, they don't rewrite the rule book yearly.

Academicians. This group is composed of those who may have worked in public education at one time for another. Academicians usually work in institutions whose operational procedures are characterized by a curious combination of anarchy, obsolescence, and self-interest. Members of this group receive institutional rewards for studying *other* institutions.

National Groups and Associations. These groups are diverse, but each exists for the purpose of providing services to the membership. Initially, almost all these groups and associations ignored the reform movement. With the advent of broad-scale legislative initiatives, their "let's ride this out" philosophy changed to a posture directed toward "cutting the losses" through joining coalitions and issuing reports—reports which often cited research favorable to the group.

The United States Department of Education. This organization had significant impact with the publication of a report titled *A Nation at Risk.* This volume implied that, "What schools are doing is not working, so we need more of it . . . better." The publication brought education to the national forefront. As the reform movement began to ebb, the department lost the opportunity for positive leadership by supporting unpopular causes and by assuming a negative posture for policy advocacy.

What does all of this have to do with teacher evaluation? It's simple! The one finding which all reformers agreed upon is that effective change occurs when initiated from the local level. Of course, as soon as they agreed on this premise, most violated it immediately through supporting "top-down" efforts at change. Evaluation is the tool for change, and it works like this—schools can demonstrate what is important by evaluating it. Teachers tend to accomplish clearly articulated goals, particularly if the goals are supported by research and staff development.

Teacher Empowerment

This term has been so overused that its meaning is almost lost. To some, teacher empowerment means replacing the principal. Consequently, the concept of teacher empowerment is seen as a threat. Administrators have seen authority taken by the legislature and bureaucrat. Now the thrust toward teacher empowerment is seen as continuing the process, but from the "bottom-up." First-line administrators feel trapped in the middle and feel they are losing authority in all directions.

Some facts about teacher empowerment are these:

1. Many of those who advocate empowerment have no idea of how this could work from a practical standpoint.
2. There is no consensus as to the definition of empowerment, except for the vague expectation that teachers should be involved in the decisions which affect their work.
3. In the best sense, teacher empowerment is little more than good administrative practice. Those working in the classroom frequently know more about the problems of effective teaching. Why would an administrator not utilize the best and most knowledgeable persons available? Very often, these persons are classroom teachers.

It is suspected that those who are opposed to empowerment of teachers are not reacting to the concept, but to poor policy. In localities where relations between administrators and teachers are already stormy, such policies simply serve as a wedge for further discord.

Empowerment is only effective when teachers and administrators work together, when parameters are set for involvement and decision making, and when each party is willing to respect the other. Earlier, it was stated that teachers could benefit from in-service on involvement. This is due to the fact that, for some teacher's, anything less than "calling the shot" is not viewed as being involved or having input. Learning that input can be significant, even with parameters, is important.

In the end, both parties must be commited to instructional decisions based upon research and valid data. When personal interest can give way to the knowledge base, official position is of less consequence. Administrators must understand that power is not a limited commodity, but expands as it is shared.

What are the opportunities to initiate change in education? As an answer to this question, let us state, "The opportunities have never been better." Most efforts at "top down" change have had marginal results, at best. The prognosis for "bottom up" change is excellent. To review a summary of the prescription for change advocated in this book, refer to Figure 10-1.

It is noteworthy that additional finances are not mentioned in Figure 10-1. Money will buy top quality teachers, and it will help to retain those teachers. It will allow the appropriate maintenance of school plant and the acquisition of high quality teaching materials and technology. Therefore, its importance cannot be diminished. It should be noted, however, that there is tremendous opportunity for change and improvement in the most meager of circumstances, since education is a human endeavor. The reliance on dollars to solve problems of commitment, measurement, expectancies, evaluation of personnel, system focus, and other problems is simply shortsighted.

It is through local commitment utilizing research-based teaching practices that positive change in education can occur. In the end, it will be the LEA's—this is the opprobrious acronym for school systems that is used by bureaucrats who seek to appear too busy to waste words or paper—who have the real opportunity to make a difference for future citizens.

Peer Observers

The use of peer observers or evaluators has much to offer in an attempt to improve the evaluation process. Peer evaluators will work best with the following guidelines:

1. If formative evaluation and summative evaluation are separated, and if peer assessors work only with formative areas
2. If a positive protocol is used in peer assessment
3. If multiple opportunities are provided for teachers to demonstrate the desired teaching practices
4. If teachers have access to more than one peer assessor
5. If both peers and administrators are trained in the use of peer assessors and in methods of peer assessment
6. If teachers are trained in the areas which are evaluated

Pay for Performance

An outgrowth of an excellent system of evaluation is the pay for performance system. When a differentiated pay system is based on an obsolete evaluation program, it is bound to fail. The evaluation system must be viewed by the teaching staff as fair and equitable, and as measuring what it is supposed to measure. Once these goals are accomplished, a differentiated pay system can be considered. The advantages of a differentiated pay system are as follows:

1. Highly motivated teachers can secure recognition and advancement without leaving the classroom.
2. Through the training programs necessary for the differentiated pay program, a significant number of teachers can become involved in focusing on effective teaching practices.
3. The differentiated pay programs can help to change the organizational climate in a school.
4. There is considerable public relations value in a differentiated pay program.

Some of the basic operational procedures and "rules of the game" are as follows:

1. Success is experienced if the differentiated pay system is based upon the formative evaluation program.
2. Don't set maximums; make the differentiated pay open to all.
3. Don't ruin the program with too much money. The goal is not competition, but cooperation.
4. Tie the differentiated pay program to the goals of the school system.
5. Involve everyone affected by the differentiated pay program in the planning process.
6. As the program is upgraded or modified, keep original purposes in the forefront. There is a tendency to co-opt a program with upgrades or modification.
7. Train everyone involved, and use in-house experts—this builds morale.

CONFERENCING

The evaluation system is almost totally dependent upon the conferencing skills of the evaluator. It is of little avail to have excellent observation if the teacher who was observed becomes alienated or disillusioned during the conferencing process. There are several rules for conferencing which help to ensure success. These are noted below:

1. Identify the purposes of the conference well in advance.
2. Adopt strategies consistent with the type of conference to be conducted.

3. Remove self from the process. Focus on the other person's needs and the purposes of the conference.

4. As the conference is completed, summarize the results, commitments, or decisions made.

5. Always set a follow-up schedule.

GO FOR THE LONG TERM

A change to improve the performance of personnel, yield better relations among administrators and teachers, improve the community's concept of schools, improve the learning of students, or anything else local planners desire for the schools, cannot be accomplished overnight. Real change requires a long-term commitment.

There is a tendency among government organizations, including education, to seek "quick fixes." The procedure of "plan, publicize, and phase-out" is well known. Bureaucracies, even small ones, however, never seem able to phase-out completely. This leaves remnants of past efforts "hanging on," with little or no benefit to the school system.

A serious effort to change should not be attempted if planners are not prepared to give at least three years—perhaps, even seven or eight years—to the effort. Leadership turnover is a problem for those planning long-term change. In many large organizations, top leadership changes frequently. For this reason, long-range change must be planned to transcend the turnover in leadership. Other suggestions for long-range planning include the following five-point checklist:

_____ **1.** Involve the school board and a broad representation from all levels.

_____ **2.** Don't give up. If one approach hits a snag, devise a new one.

_____ **3.** Articulate the vision in every conceivable way and for every conceivable constituency.

_____ **4.** Make the long-range planning dynamic: that is, be ready to incorporate new research and new structures.

_____ **5.** Set forth a multiyear checklist for various tasks and goals. (Publicize the results yearly.)

Even though local practitioners tend to point to other levels of the educational enterprise as being obstructive to change, this does not absolve practitioners from the responsibility for making schools effective. It just takes more effort, commitment, and, of course, additional local employees to respond to the deluge of memoranda, regulations, and surveys that obstruct or impose. This is one of the strange paradoxes of education—the bureaucrats and politicians inundate the local school systems with red tape and then attack local school administrators for spending funds on the support personnel required to respond. The challenge is to accomplish goals, even in adversity.

Finally, evaluation is an excellent tool for initiating change in the schools. This is true, because evaluation is more than the simple rating of teaching ability. Evaluation defines what is important in the practice of teaching. It defines the parameters for staff development, and it is the pivotal component of the curriculum delivery system. With its importance, it is amazing that evaluation remains one of the few areas which is within the control of the local school systems.

SUMMARY

The organizing principle for this text has been that an effective teacher evaluation system cannot be bought or borrowed. For evaluation to be effective, those being evaluated must have ownership and confidence in the system. This is unlikely to occur if evaluation is pulled off the shelf and implemented.

There is also a strong suspicion that the checklist approach to evaluation is possibly more destructive than helpful. Examples of checklists could be easily borrowed or bought but such exercises may be a waste of time.

The development of an effective evaluation system takes more than one year. Through the approach outlined in this book, an excellent system of evaluation can be developed.

APPENDIX

The professional personnel of the Washington County School System in Hagerstown, Maryland, has identified professional practices and performance indicators, which they call "domains, competencies, behaviors—criteria for teacher evaluation." Superintendent Richard Whisner reports that the system is piloting the evaluation system initially in just a few schools. There are plans to expand its use as additional experience is gained and additional input from the staff is received.

The Washington County effort involved in identifying the criteria for evaluation has been commendable, and there are plans to incorporate formative and summative activities into its evaluation system. This is an example whereby local personnel have recognized the research base on effective teaching and attempted to use it in a system of evaluation.

The eight professional practices and performance indicators used in Washington County are listed below in Appendix 1.A. It is noteworthy that some of the performance indicators have subsections. As suggested earlier, the teacher observers in Washington County do not attempt to observe the entire evaluation system in a single visit. It is typical for an observer to evaluate just one area per observation session.

Each of the eight professional practices is accompanied with a written narrative in order that the observer and teachers will have a common view about the behaviors sought in the evaluation. An example of the written narrative for one of the performance areas, Instructional Planning, is given in Appendix 1.B.

APPENDIX 1.A—EIGHT PROFESSIONAL PRACTICES AND THEIR PERFORMANCE INDICATORS

A. INSTRUCTIONAL PLANNING*
  1. Plans lessons and units with objectives
     a. States objectives for learner outcomes
     b. Includes objectives which meet the varied needs of learners
  2. Plans instruction to achieve objectives
     a. Matches the instructional process and subject content to Stated objectives
     b. Identified learner activities and materials for carrying out stated objectives

B. INSTRUCTIONAL DELIVERY
  3. Carries out instructional plans
     a. Teaches to established objectives
     b. Uses the planned instructional process and subject content
     c. Uses the planner learner activities and materials
     d. Adapts educational plans if unexpected situation occurs
  4. Uses and effective instructional process
     a. Establishes the focus of the lesson
     b. Reviews concepts/skills previously learned
     c. Presents clearly new concepts to be learned
     d. Assists learners in practicing new concepts/skills
     e. Provides learners an opportunity for independent practice of new concepts/skills
     f. Gives feedback to learners on attainment of new concepts/skills
  5. Uses teaching methods which respond to learner needs
     a. Teaches at varying cognitive levels
     b. Accommodates varying learner styles
     c. Paces lessons to meet learner needs
     d. Uses examples related to learner experiences
     e. Varies grouping to meet learner needs

C. CLASSROOM MANAGEMENT
  6. Organizes instructional learning time
     a. Systematizes routine procedure and tasks
     b. Teaches scheduled class/subject for allocated time period
     c. Maximizes learner equipment in instruction
  7. Uses space, equipment, and materials to support instruction
     a. Arranges the learning area to achieve planned objectives
     b. Uses equipment and materials effectively
     c. Makes materials readily accessible to learners

---

* The narrative for instructional planning is given in Appendix 1.B. As stated, a similar narrative description has been developed for all competencies and performance indicators.

8. Establishes classroom rules and routines that promote instruction
   a. Uses rules and/or routines at the developmental level of learners
   b. Applies rules and/or routines consistently
9. Manages learner student behavior effectively
   a. Communicates behavioral expectations to learners
   b. Maintains a common purpose among learners and the teachers
   c. Monitors learners' behaviors
   d. Corrects inappropriate classroom behavior

D. TEACHER-LEARNER INTERACTION
   10. Communicates high expectations for learning
       a. Expects all learners to succeed
       b. Provides all learners with an opportunity to learn
       c. Holds learners accountable for learning
   11. Engages learners in instruction
       a. Uses questions to elicit learner responses
       b. Encourages learners' questions and contributions to lessons
       c. Responds constructively to learner questions and contributions
       d. Provides activities that promote interaction among learners
   12. Uses principles of motivation
       a. Rewards learners' success
       b. Creates a pleasant learning climate
       c. Varies instructional activities to match learners' interests
       d. Creates an appropriate level of concern
       e. Makes sure students know the results of their efforts
       f. Takes advantage of intrinsic and extrinsic rewards
   13. Demonstrates exemplary communication skills
       a. Speaks and writes clearly
       b. Uses oral and written language correctly
       c. Gives clear, concise directions and explanations
       d. Matches communication to meet the purpose of instruction and learners' needs
   14. Uses principles of reinforcement
       a. Uses positive reinforcement to increase desired behavior
       b. Uses negative reinforcement (escape/avoidance) technique to increase desired behavior
       c. Uses punishment when necessary to suppress undesired behaviors
       d. Uses extinction to decrease undesirable behavior
   15. Uses principles of retention and transfer
       a. Promotes meaning to relating instruction to students' lives and experiences
       b. Makes use of feeling tone
       c. Promotes transfer so students can use what they have previously learned
       d. Uses a schedule of practice for new and review material
       e. Makes sure that students have learned the basic information well

      f.   Uses association to make students aware of meanings that apply to new information

      g. Uses similarity to teach students new concepts and skills

      h. Uses the identification of critical elements to promote retention and transfer

E. SUBJECT CONTENT

   16. Shows command of subject matter

      a. Demonstrates mastery of subject knowledge and skills

      b. Presents information that is accurate and up-to-date

      c. Communicates information from a bias-free, multicultural perspective

      d. Uses a variety of subject matter resources

   17. Communicates major concepts and principles of subject matter

      a. Organizes subject matter into meaningful lesson(s)

      b. Relates specific lesson topics to major subject matter concepts and generalizations

      c. Incorporates recognized (or required) curricular guidelines into lessons

F. EVALUATION

   18. Evaluates learner performance

      a. Assesses prior learning

      b. Monitors ongoing performance of learners

      c. Encourages learners to evaluate their own performance

      d. Evaluates learner's achievement of stated objective

      e. Uses a variety of evaluation techniques

   19. Uses evaluation results

      a. Uses evaluation to give learners timely feedback on performance

      b. Uses evaluation to diagnose learning difficulties

      c. Uses evaluation to plan/adapt instruction

G. PROFESSIONAL RESPONSIBILITIES

   20. Engages in professional growth activities that relate to classroom performance

      a. Pursues knowledge about current thinking, trends, and practices in education

      b. Teacher is flexible in approach to teaching

   21. Demonstrates dependability in professional duties

      a. Fulfills assigned tasks

      b. Is prompt

   22. Works cooperatively in bringing about the success of the school program

      a. Cooperates with others to bring about the success of the school program

      b. Exhibits a professional responsibility of the physical and material resources that support the instructional program

      c. Helps to communicate the purposes of the school's program to the community

H. PROFESSIONAL RELATIONSHIPS
    23. Maintains an effective working relationship with staff
      a. Respects needs and feelings of his/her colleagues
      b. Maintains a positive relationship with all school personnel
    24. Maintains a relationship with students that is conducive to learning
      a. Maintains a supportive and positive relationship with students
      b. Respects the confidentiality of student information
    25. Maintains a relationship with parents that promotes effective communication
      a. Maintains rapport with parents
      b. Is available for conferences
      c. Shows tack in communication

Definitions of Rating Scale Levels

Outstanding. Performance in this area is consistently effective; teaching practices are superior. Teaching behaviors are demonstrated at the highest level of performance.

Competent. Performance in this area is generally effective. Teaching practices are at a consistently acceptable level. Supervision and assistance may be offered in order for the teacher to have the opportunity to achieve at a higher level of performance.

Unsatisfactory. Performance in this area is ineffective. The teacher needs more development or assistance to maintain an acceptable level. The teacher requires supervision and assistance to attain competence.

APPENDIX 1.B—INSTRUCTIONAL PLANNING

Planning is part of the basic decision-making process in which a teacher visualizes the future, inventories the means and ends of educational activities, and designs a framework to guide his or her action. Part of the decision-making process involves the selection of appropriate objectives, activities, and materials for lessons, units, and courses. The ability not only to plan but also to implement and adapt a plan (as appropriate) is essential for effective teaching. Plans might be viewed as flexible frameworks for action, a way of starting in the right direction, but also something from which a teacher might depart or elaborate. Evidences of planning may be observed during classroom visitations, found in written plans, or discussed during a teacher conference. Plans are only as good as the instruction they promote. Extensive research exists which identifies characteristics of effective instruction.

Research has focused on how teachers organize and plan instruction. Other investigations have sought to identify a number of events which seem to characterize quality instruction, and effective teaching is organized around such events. Several well-known lesson models are built on this information (e.g., Active Teaching, Hunter's Model Lesson) and are often labeled as direct instruction approaches. Selection of a lesson model should be based on the type of learning outcome desired and the prior learning of the students to be taught. Direct instruction models promote increased achievement test scores, while other models are better at promoting creativity and problem-solving competencies, independence, curiosity, and positive attitudes towards school. Furthermore, research indicates that choice of instructional strategy should depend upon the student and his or her needs and learning style.

A. INSTRUCTIONAL PLANNING*
1. Plans lessons and units with objectives
    Objectives are the critical beginnings for achieving desired student outcomes. Clear statements of objectives describe a desired state in the learner and succeed in communicating that intent to others. Clear objectives are often expressed in behavioral terms. Objectives become part of a teacher's mental image of what occurs during instruction.
    a. States objectives for learner outcomes
        The observer:
        • Hears the teacher tell the purpose of a new lesson to the learners
        • Hears the teacher review the connection of today's lesson to previous activities
        • Reviews the learners' course outline
        • Anticipates outcomes of a future lesson
        • Reviews written plans
    b. Includes objectives which meet the varied needs of learners
        The observer:
        • Asks the teacher how a lesson/objective has been modified for learners with special needs (e.g., handicaps, ability levels)
        • Watches/listens to the teacher to note alternative/adapted assignments/for requirements given to learners
        • Looks for tutoring or individual / small group instruction of learners
        • Reviews written notes or plans for evidence of varied objectives
2. Plans instruction to achieve objectives
    After a teacher selects appropriate learner outcomes, he or she must decide what instructional methods will best achieve such ends. Teachers should plan only activities that specifically carry out the objectives.
    a. Matches the instructional process and subject content to stated objectives
        The Observer:

---

* Note that for purposes of clarity, the numeration has been changed, so that it is consistent in Appendix 1.A and 1.B.

- Notes if there are learner objectives for each step of any established lesson / instructional model
- Notes the logical sequence of objectives in a written lesson plan (e.g., easy to difficult)
- Notes that the subject content presented is tied to specific learner outcomes
- Checks lesson plans for subject content which matches the objectives

b. Identifies learner activities and materials for carrying out stated objectives

The observer:

- Checks to see if all stated objectives in a lesson plan have appropriate learning activities
- Reviews lesson plans and notes whether materials for each activity are specified (as appropriate)
- Observes what materials have been set out for upcoming activity

BIBLIOGRAPHY

American Association of School Executives, *Effective Teaching: Observations from Research,* 1801 North Moore Street, Arlington, Virginia 22209, 1986.

Broyles, Norman L., and Denise Vrchota, *Performance-Based Compensation Model: Status and Potential for Implementation,* Iowa Association of School Boards, Insurance Exchange Building #927, 505 Fifth Avenue, Des Moines, Iowa 50309-2316, November 1986.

Cohen, David, and Richard J. Murnane, "Merits of Merit Pay," *The Public Interest,* No. 80, Summer 1985. Copies may be obtained from Stanford Educational Policy Institute, Stanford University.

Commonwealth of Virginia, Department of Education, *Beginning Teacher Assistance Program,* Richmond, Virginia 23216, 1986.

Glasser, William, M.D., *Control Therapy in the Classroom,* New York: Perennial Library, Harper and Row, 1986.

Good, Thomas L., and Jere E. Brophy, *Looking in Classrooms,* New York: Harper and Row, 1984.

Goodlad, John, *A Place Called School,* New York: McGraw-Hill, 1983.

Harris, Louis, and Associates, *The American Teacher,* New York, A Survey Conducted for Metropolitan Life Insurance, 1986.

Hiscor, Susan, March Braverman, Warren Evans, et al., *How to Increase Learning Time: A Tool for Teachers,* Portland, Oregon: Northwest Regional Education Laboratory, 1982.

Hunter, Madeline, *Mastery Teaching,* El Segundo, California: T.I.P. Publications, 1982.

Johnson, Nancy C., and J. Kenneth Orso, "Teacher Evaluation Criteria," *Spectrum: Journal of School Research and Information,* Vol. 4, No. 3, Arlington, Virginia: Educational Research Service, Inc., Summer 1986.

Jondt, Fred Edmund, and Paul Gillette, *Win-Win Negotiating: Turning Conflict into Agreement,* New York: John Wiley and Sons, 1985.

National School Public Relations Association, *Good Teachers: What to Look For,* Arlington, Virginia, 1981.

Northwest Regional Educational Laboratory, *Outcome-based Education.* For an introduction about the work of those involved in Outcome-Based Education, contact the Northwest Regional Education Laboratory, 300 S.W. Sixth Avenue, Portland, Oregon 97204.

Orange County Public Schools, *Assessment for Professional Development,* Orange, Virginia 22960, July 1986.

Rouche, John E., and George A. Baker, III, *Profiling Excellence in America's Schools,* Arlington, Virginia: American Association of School Administrators, 1986.

U.S. Department of Education, *What Works: Research about Teaching and Learning,* Washington, D.C., 1986.

Washington County Public Schools, *Domains, Competencies, and Behaviors: Criteria For Teacher Evaluation,* Hagerstown, Maryland 21740, 1987.

Wise, Arthur, Linda Darling-Hammond, et al. *Teacher Evaluation, A Study of Effective Practices,* prepared for the National Institute of Education by the Rand Corp, 1700 Main Street, P. O. Box 2138, Santa Monica, California 90406-2138, 1985.

INDEX